Unfortunately, many single Christians watch the world go by in pairs, inwardly protesting, "God, what about me?" Janet Fix once bemoaned loneliness as her life sentence. But personal experience and biblical truth convinced her that "there must be a way to live in the freedom and joy of the Lord without the heavy clouds of incompleteness hanging overhead." FOR SINGLES ONLY confidently asserts that God intended the "abundant life" for singles as well as couples, for the here and now as well as the hereafter. The author encourages you to pursue—and shows you how to find—the genuine fulfillment available to every individual willing to submit to the Bridegroom.

FOR SINGLES ONLY

Janet Fix

With Zola Levitt

Fleming H. Revell Company
Old Tappan, New Jersey

Library of Congress Cataloging in Publication Data

Fix, Janet.
  For singles only.

  1. Single people—Religious life. I. Levitt, Zola,
joint author. II. Title.
BV4596.S5F58   248′.84   78-9754
ISBN 0-8007-5034-9

With love and deep gratitude
to my parents, brothers, and sister,
whose love and support
taught me the truth of Romans 8:28.

Contents

FOR SINGLES ONLY

•

1

Happiness—How to Get It, How to Use it

I'm like you. I want to be happy.

I'm an American, and my Constitution says I have the *right* to pursue happiness. I'm a Christian, and my Gospel promises me the abundant life. My Lord said that He told us all these things ". . . that your joy might be full" (John 15:11 KJV).

And I'm like you in the respect that I often ask, "What's in it for me?" I have my selfish moments, like you, and I frequently study situations in my life with the attitude "Will it make me *happy?*"

Something's wrong somewhere.

The United States has achieved accomplishments and stature that place us first among nations in some very important areas, it's true. But even though our Constitution has guaranteed our right to pursue happiness, and our Bible says it is ours for the asking, few of us have achieved it.

Something is either wrong with our guarantees or with us. If I had a guarantee on a house plant or a car or a watch that turned out to be as so-so as this "abundant life," I'd take the thing back. That is, I'd take it back if I had properly watered it, given it its regular maintenance, or wound it properly.

Of course human beings are a bit more complex than the

13

average merchandise that comes our way in this world. Sometimes people who talk to their plants (or cars, or watches) get better results than when they talk to people. People are complex. People are a great mystery to other people, and they have given God some rough moments, too.

Among the people who must give God some of His most trying days are those called *singles*.

Because we singles are especially vulnerable to the disappointments and anxieties that come with unfulfilled pursuits and guarantees, we become self-centered in our singleness, thinking we have a monopoly on loneliness and broken dreams. It's easy to feel cheated or think that God has failed us because we're single.

I know, because I concluded when I was twenty-five that life had passed me by and that the remainder of my days was a sort of prison sentence that I must serve. I was one of those Christians who had decided that the "abundant life" was the next life; it just couldn't be *this one.* Surely God had something fine set up for me in the Kingdom to come, because it was obvious He didn't have much for me in the here and now. *What treasures He must have in store for me,* I exulted, as I examined my earthly pittance.

I was a good girl, and I set out to find God's will on how to be happy. I studied the Christian psychologists' tomes which told single women how to function in the church and how to live a happy but unmarried life.

Every book seemed to tell me to *do* something. The idea was to transfer my passions and my energies to worthwhile charitable or church activities. Lord knows I had romantic desire enough to spare, but the books said it could be rechanneled into God's service, and I would be happy.

And if what those books advised really did make single girls happy, I should have been the happiest single good girl in the whole church. I was already *doing* things. I was doing all the things good girls do and not doing all the things good girls are not supposed to do, and between what I was doing and what I was not doing, I led a very active life.

But doing didn't make me happy. I was sad and lonely, and felt God had cheated me, even after all I'd done for Him. I really believed He had reneged on His guarantees.

I finally told God, "Lord, I'm a church secretary, I direct the junior choir, I sing in the regular choir, I teach the high-school Sunday-school class, and I sponsor the junior-high youth fellowship. I like these things, but they aren't filling that void.

"I'm tired. I'm lonely. I feel as if I'm married to the church, and I didn't even take the vows, and I don't wear the habit."

I had to admit that my activities did give me real pleasure, but not a lasting sense of fulfillment and happiness. When the activities stopped, I was left rather empty and alone. I couldn't keep my busywork going twenty-four hours a day, so I always ended up with some lonely time to spare. Depression and frustration set in. I realized that I was only running on a treadmill and trying to please God so much that He would finally get around to answering my prayers. I started to take things into my own hands. I quit acting as the resident saint and began to experiment with life. I stretched some horizons a bit, convinced that happiness must lie somewhere out there where I had never reached before.

That was disaster!

Mark me down for a couple of broken engagements, financial ruin, endless job changes, and a newly bitter attitude toward God.

I ended up thinking, "I've prayed, and I haven't received. Why pray anymore?"

But eventually, as you can well imagine, I made the inevitable journey home.

What else could I do? As the disciples admitted, there was nowhere else to go. He *does* have the answers, and now that

I've grown a little more in Him, I'm the first to enjoy them.

My sojourn into the world I hadn't known before did teach me some vital facts: My general discontent was not a rare disease, and whatever was wrong with me must be inward, because I wasn't happy in my "freedom" either. In fact, I found unhappiness everywhere I went, and it was as virulent among marrieds as it was among singles. My experience in the end showed only that I was being natural, and that feelings of discontent are simply part of the human condition—especially when one takes life into his own control.

I learned that people associate happiness with some other person, vaguely defined, who might one day come along and provide it. Or happiness might be involved with some object or goal: money, love, children. But anyway, it's widely regarded as something very elusive which comes upon one out of pure luck.

The married woman might think happiness lies in her home, her husband, or in some particular behavior on the part of her children. The married man looks for happiness in a prettier, more lively woman, a new car, a boat, golf, and on and on.

Interestingly, many marrieds say, "If only I could be single," and singles say, "If only I could be married."

The dictionary speaks of *happy* as "happenstance, luck, or good fortune." The secular definition intensifies that feeling of the fortunate accident making our lives happy. But to me that's a hazardous way to look at life. I'm all for happy accidents and the optimistic fortune-cookie fulfillment, but I'd hate to have my sense of peace and well-being depend on them.

Now it's true, our common sense tells us, that circumstances around us do determine our sense of well-being. Fat people would rather be slender; plain people would rather be beautiful; sick people would rather be healthy. Each person seems to have his pet list of shortcomings right at his fingertips (while the list of blessings is usually lost somewhere in the broken-dreams file). As a result, most people are truly very anxious about life.

But happiness is not determined by a scale which balances blessings against bad breaks.

The apostle Paul, a single person who wrote much of the New Testament, was one Bible writer whose feelings showed. Even unbelievers concede that Paul was genuine flesh and blood. His writing is personal, highly spiritual, and very practical. He lived a tough life, mostly as the unwanted messenger, among strangers, of unwanted Good News. He was run out of many towns, whipped, imprisoned, and abused for his troubles. He had reason to be as anxious about life as any one of us is today.

And yet he wrote, "Be anxious for nothing . . ." (Philippians 4:6 NAS).

Great!

There's the answer, we might say with a wry attitude. But it's a hard one to swallow. Can I really be anxious for nothing?

Paul went on in that Scripture ". . . but in everything by prayer and supplication with thanksgiving let your requests be made known to God" (NAS).

We tend to get so concerned with our illnesses that we forget to take the medicine. We particularly forget the part about "thanksgiving." Paul is frank. He knows we have needs and problems, and that anxieties will try to take their toll from each of us. But he answers that prayer and supplication—with thanksgiving—will relieve the anxieties.

If we have taken everything to God with prayer and thanksgiving, we gain the greatest possible state of being, "the peace of God that passes all understanding." Paul was never unrealistic or irresponsible; he meant exactly what he said. We are to be carefree—really free of all care. We are to be "anxious for nothing." He doesn't say there will be no problems, just no anxieties.

It sounds a bit superficial, doesn't it? The natural mind *wants* to have cares—anxieties. "My marital status is important," you may say, and it certainly is. But what we tend to do with our obsessive cares is pretty much what I did. We go out and search around, in mad pursuit of a happiness that may well be outside God's design for us altogether. We try to help God answer our prayers by setting ourselves up for the answers we seek, and all we're really doing is taking God's prerogatives into our own hands.

Perhaps in our heart of hearts we think God *owes* us some happiness (some of what *we* think is happiness), since we're Christians, "good" girls or boys, and dedicated to doing His things. We lean on our own understanding, and we tend to go round and round, always compelled to search, but never really finding anything.

I myself have been there, I can assure you, and while I may not be able to save you the trouble of the trip, I can at least tell you what I found out. The parties, the illicit sex, the changing of jobs, the moving of apartments, and all the rest of the "grab it while you can" work for nobody.

In this book we'll look into a lot of the Bible and a lot of the problems of contemporary life as well. We'll discuss sex, to begin with; the tremendous emotions that we all have within us; the broken heart and how it can be fixed; the whole matter of love; masturbation; homosexuality; "liberation" of all sorts; and finally, reality—living with "what is."

I work with singles a great deal now. This is my major ministry. In my seminars, in my own church, and, most importantly, in my personal life, I have gathered some facts of interest and some experiences that I think will be helpful. I'm not a psychologist or a pastor or even an especially gifted counselor. But what I'll share works. He did it for me, so I know He can do it for you.

By the time we finish, we can experience together, "I can do all things through Christ which strengtheneth me" (Philippians 4:13 KJV). And really believe "But my God shall supply all your need according to his riches in glory by Christ Jesus" (Philippians 4:19 KJV).

This is the life God has guaranteed in His original plan. We can be free of care and anxiety, full of the peace which passes all understanding, and content in any state we happen to find ourselves.

I suppose my major qualification for talking with you about this subject is this: I'm single, and I'm happy. You can be happy this way too. Read on.

2
Consenting Adults

Most self-help books for singles, or for anyone else for that matter, put the chapter on sex in the back of the book. That's seemingly supposed to indicate that sex is unimportant or embarrassing.

That's not my view.

Sex is important in almost everybody's life, including the lives of singles. Single Christian people are in a very tough position as far as sex is concerned, and there's no getting away from that. The Bible treats the subject frankly and decisively, and I believe what it says. But in the "new morality," that puts me in the position of being a "consenting adult" who is never supposed to consent.

If you are single, past puberty, and a believer, you're in that position too. And since I assume I'm talking to mature adults and not dating teenagers, I think we can dispense with talk of the birds and the bees and face life as it faces us.

I guess it all starts with the date. So I'm going to take off somewhat from my own life again, if you'll bear with me, beginning with my first date (which you probably won't drool over). I won't be revealing the whole of my thoughts or my life experiences to you, but I want to share some valuable lessons I've learned.

Come back with me now to those thrilling days of yesteryear when the twelve-year-old Janet got asked out!

My parents did not actually allow me to date at that early age, but they made an exception for this event. My "escort" was the son of a local Baptist minister, and he brought his parents and sister along. Rather, they brought him! His father drove, and I had to sit in front with his parents while he sat in the backseat with his sister. To make sure that I knew it wasn't a *real* date, my mother insisted that I pay for my own ticket. Since we were going to the harmless Youth for Christ Sweetheart Banquet, my parents were correct in assuming there would be no hanky-panky. Besides, I was scared!

It took me a year to recover—in time for the next annual Sweetheart Banquet. It was a good two years beyond that when I began actual dating (where nobody brought his parents or his sister).

Some people think of dating as hunting, and it is, in a way. The Christian men are looking for a bride among the Bride of Christ, hopefully, and women become fishers of men in a very real sense.

The Bible says nothing about dating. Dating isn't scriptural, but it's not unscriptural either. Common sense tells us that dating is a necessary prelude to being married, and that it is a natural, meaningful human endeavor. In Bible days people got married by contract—that is, they made an agreement before the fact—and it stands to reason that they must have courted in order to at least establish the terms of the contract. In ancient Israel a bride price was paid by the groom to the bride's father; it figures he'd had some time with the bride in a "dating" situation in order that he could place a value on her. He had to make a sacrifice in order to have the bride, and thus he must have been reasonably acquainted with her as a person.

Dating today is probably largely what it was in biblical Israel: the effort to achieve a relationship worthy of a solid contract. It is preparation for marriage, the elimination of less-than-contract material, and the discovery of much joy and fulfillment. It is fun. It is a maturing and broadening experience. It can be a spiritually rejuvenating activity. On the part of Christian people, it is to be a Christ-centered experience and a very important one.

Many of our own personal methods for successful dating are, consciously or unconsciously, related to the sexual realm. We qualify our dating partners in subtle and sophisticated ways, usually quickly eliminating those who somehow don't appeal to us physically, and we go through quite a bit of trouble to make ourselves physically attractive. No one in his right mind would go out for an evening looking terrible, of course, but it's remarkable how far we tend to go the other way. Men buy expensive suits, get fancy haircuts, even purchase high-priced cars, jewelry, and the like; women restyle their hair, buy clothing according to an important partner's taste, and even attempt to change their whole personalities, on occasion, to suit a date.

All well and good. This is very human, if a bit unreliable. The very act of our representing ourselves at our best is a good thing. To the degree that we become phony, of course, all this gilding of the lily is phony too. But normally people are still who they are, even when they look terrific and smell exceptionally good.

Women tend to set up evenings of romance in the manner that football teams set up special plays. Everything is in its right position—dinner, soft music, and so forth—and the subject is supposed to be unaware that he is the star of the whole show.

It feels good to be secure in a comfortable setting. The natural sequence of events can quickly activate the strong forces of "gland power," which so easily lead to an emotion-

packed physical relationship. And because we're no longer
children, it is easy to put away childish things and believe
we've become "consenting adults."

It is important to realize that we happen to live in a social
system that absolutely dictates against a single man or woman
remaining chaste. Sex is "natural" these days. And "natural"
is "in."

We haven't invented anything new. "Swinging" is as old as
Sodom and Gomorrah, and the Samaritan woman would be
right at home in our present culture.

It's no secret that we have huge industries operating that
traffic in the rawest forms of sexual expression. In fact, we have
probably far exceeded Sodom and Gomorrah by modernizing
sex technically, so that it now appears on movie screens, the
TV, and in widely circulated books. In Dallas, the public can
now order a home movie, X-rated, along with projector and
nude projectionist. In Los Angeles, perverse sexual practices
that would have once horrified a psychoanalyst are available
for hire through newspaper ads. Midtown New York seems
utterly devoted to satisfying the sexual delectations of a host of
tourists and natives, with every other marquee offering a more
titillating thrill than the last. No matter how you like it, you can
have it more profusely than ever before. C. S. Lewis in *Mere
Christianity* puts it very well: "We grow up surrounded by
propaganda in favor of unchastity. There are people who want
to keep our sex instinct inflamed in order to make money out
of us. Because, of course, a man with an obsession is a man
who has very little sales resistance."

This affects the whole fabric of society. The very sight of
these sexual advertisements depresses those adverse to them,
but it also makes a certain dent in their philosophy. Enough
exposure to the sexually oriented forces, and the mind starts to
be manipulated into accepting behavior that once was con-
sidered wrong. Lonely people exposed to the daily prolifera-

tion of sex, who are led to believe that "everybody's doing it," quickly begin to question the value of the Christian standards they have been taught. It is clear that the Christian community is being affected by this particular direction of our society.

I really believe what pornography appeals to in people is not so much their sex drive but their loneliness and frustrated emptiness. Lonely people reach out for expressions of love; that's just how we're put together. The mind will accept sex in many forms as a cure for loneliness, because it seems to work—at least temporarily. At heart, people want to be close, to be held. And sex provides closeness and embraces. Premarital or extramarital sex doesn't really provide a very permanent loneliness antidote, of course, but often desperation will cause one to believe that "beggars can't be choosers."

The lonely person will seemingly give *anything* to avoid more loneliness. He will reach out for an expression of love—wherever it is and however he can get it. Somehow the mind convinces itself that sex is really love. "It can't be sin, because we're in love, and we'll get married eventually," goes one soothing rationalization. "If I don't, he'll think I'm a prude, and I'll lose him," agonizes the lonely woman. Portia Nelson puts it this way, "If I say 'no' to you, I will lose you. If I say 'yes' . . . I will lose myself. Even if I win, I lose . . . ."

This doesn't apply only to singles, of course. Most singles, Christians included, have been approached by lonely married people for companionship and more. "My wife [husband] doesn't understand me," goes the line, and it's sometimes truly the case. The single's heart is moved (or loneliness assuaged or lust provoked or hostility awakened), and an unfortunate affair takes place, which time and again leads to real disaster.

One of the most difficult jolts of my life was the first time a Christian married man made a very definite proposition to me and actually suggested an affair. He was a well-known gospel

singer, and I assumed he didn't have a problem in the world—
least of all a marital problem. I was young and hadn't yet
learned some of the facts of life.

I'm older now, and I know that sexual sin goes on among
Christians—married and single. Apparently God said what He
did about this subject in the Scriptures because people needed
the guidance. We certainly don't go around boasting about
fornication and adultery—that wouldn't be Christian—but it's
done all the same. I know I don't speak for everyone, of
course, nor am I necessarily speaking for myself; but Christians
sin—as much as we pretend we don't.

Most Christians do not seek out sin. Most Christians want to
avoid this kind of sin, and they make a real effort to avoid it.
But Christians, like non-Christians, sometimes get into desperate circumstances. Depression, loneliness, and pure lust are
not the exclusive provinces of the unbeliever. The Bible uses
the term *stumble* in connection with sin, and that does express
what happens to us. We try to walk the straight and narrow,
but now and then we stumble.

God understands the stumbling of His children. That's why
He went to so much trouble to make a provision for our sin
and offers forgiveness with: "I will remember their sin no
more!"

In spite of some of our reasoning, God said what He did
about this subject because sex is very special and important in
a human relationship, and in order to make it all He intended it
to be, we need guidance. Guidance from Him!

There are some very definite Scriptures about fornication
and adultery, and probably every unmarried, and married,
Christian has read them.

They can be downright frightening, especially to the lonely
and confused. The Seventh Commandment is succinct. The
declarations in Ephesians 5 and 1 Corinthians 5 and 6 that say
that those who commit these sexual sins have no inheritance in

the Kingdom of God are horrifying to believers who sin. Fornication and adultery are listed by the Lord in the same place as murder, and people who do these things will not see God—that's what He said.

The loopholes and exceptions aren't there. I know. I looked for them.

Time and again, wherever I go, people ask me why God comes down so hard against sex outside of marriage. At times, to some people, God seems most unreasonable and unrealistic to require such strict abstinence.

In my own search of the Scriptures, I arrived at the fact that God is not against sex. He created sex, and He created male and female, and He saw that it was good! Fornication is termed by Paul as "a sin against his [one's] own body," because our sexual natures are vital to us and to God. God intended the sexual relationship to be so much more than a fleeting erotic sensation; His purpose is our ultimate well-being, the bringing together of two minds and hearts in a prototype of heavenly love and sacrifice. Sex is not just a physical union, but an expression of the union of what in us is humanity, life, and God's ultimate creation.

Theologian Dr. Dwight Hervey Small says, in his *The Right To Remarry:*

> . . . [sex] is symbolic of the total union of persons—mind, spirit, and body. So intimate is the sexual union when it is fused with love and commitment, that it is the unique carrier of emotional and spiritual meanings of marriage. It symbolizes as nothing else can the exclusive commitment of two people to each other. The biblical perspective is that marriage needs sex, and sex needs marriage, and both need to be fused in the bonds of man's spirit. God has appointed sexual intercourse within marriage to be the sign and symbol of intimate union.

And Dr. Small concludes, advisedly, "It is, after all, God's prerogative to appoint what He will, and this He has appointed."

When this union of body, soul, and spirit can be shared and carried out to the full extent and meaning of the commitment, we have the very definition of marriage—marriage as God made it at the very creation. Sex pervades all aspects of life and affects the mind, the soul, and the body. When the union cannot be fulfilled in all aspects of life, frustration and turmoil take over—not only in the mind, but the body and the spirit.

Human beings don't come in separate pieces. We are a complete trichotomy; one part can't be categorized or isolated from another. That's why Scripture says fornication is not only a sin against another, but against self. Within an individual, sexual intercourse begins a natural process that affects the glands, emotions, and instincts of commitment and "oneness." Individuals involved in promiscuous sex are trying to make it involve the body only, and that's impossible. Consequently, damage is done to the parts of the being that are cut off from the natural fulfillment which sex is intended to bring. Nerves and emotions must be thwarted and seared in order to keep on indulging, and we're forced to become less than whole, with our sensitivities crippled.

Contrary to popular opinion, sex outside marriage is not natural. It is natural for a man and woman to have sexual intercourse, but not without giving oneself completely to the other. Most promiscuous lovers are not ready to completely give or to completely receive.

That sort of brings us back to dating. Dating leads up to marriage, the way we approach it today, and so the devil does some of his most energetic work with people who are involved in a courtship. Obviously, people who are seeing each other again and again in romantic settings, putting their best feet forward, and heading hopefully toward the altar together make an easy target. They're excited. They're working on a true union, increasingly, and their normal desires surface during the "dating game."

How "far" should people go in the dating situation?

I can't say for anyone else.

I'm not an authority and don't know, but I can safely say this: Each individual can definitely feel his or her inner transmission shift into overdrive. At a given point in each relationship, friendship starts becoming desire, and desire passion, and passion lust. As surely as we know when we're hungry for food, we know when we're hungry for sex. You know when you've reached the point of no return!

Sex is so designed that one experience automatically leads to another, almost like a drug addict becomes hooked to his temporary highs. Temporary satisfaction in a nonmarried sexual relationship naturally creates a desire for more. The appetite for sex is merely whetted, not satisfied.

Of course we know that sexual relations are not just an expression of love. God intended this expression not only to unite two individuals, but to be the means to create new life. What better atmosphere for a new baby than the love of a perfect union? How tragic that thousands of babies are born into imperfect unions, and worse yet, that babies are brought into no union at all.

But today abortion has become a common way to avoid the responsibility of motherhood. Since it is not natural to have only one parent, the woman will do just about anything to avoid having a child out of wedlock. Usually the pregnancy ends in death—either the death of the unborn child, or suicide for the unwed mother.

Yes, we have the pill, and yes, we have abortion, but the two together just show how unnatural we must be to act "natural" with our sex. If women must prevent or kill the life within them, something is terribly wrong.

Now, of course, all this dramatic data does not speak to the fact that folks who are courting experience tremendous emotional intensity. Who's thinking about pills and abortions when the moon is full and the lover is near? Helmut Thielicke, in his *The Ethics of Sex,* points out that:

> There are far more oaths [of eternal love] sworn on park benches on summer nights than on the witness stands of the courts. Why is it that a full moon and the scent of roses should turn the formula of an oath into everyday speech? After all, everybody knows that such oaths are usually broken.

That's true. Thinking people know that those oaths of undying love spoken in moments of passion "tend to cool in the warmth of the sun." Everyday life has a way of coming back the following morning and, so the pop tune says it, "The Thrill Is Gone."

But we love to hear them so much that we're willing to believe. We're willing to think he or she really means it, even when the stakes are so terribly high. We're willing, somehow, to gamble with life itself—our own and possibly our child's. It's not only our glands that go awry; we're perfectly willing to bend our brains around until they aren't even working right, just to believe in those romantic oaths.

There is nothing more devastating for a single woman than to face marriage and motherhood with someone she really doesn't love, because there's a baby on the way. Even people of the "new morality" don't recommend any of the above. They recommend that you be smart enough not to get caught; but there's no foolproof way, that is, except for total abstinence.

Abstinence isn't very popular either, but any guy or gal who has been forced into loveless marriage, or the loved ones of a girl who has had an abortion or lost her life will tell you that abstinence is the better alternative.

It is no shock to me to encounter quite frequently a Christian woman or girl who has had an abortion. It has become the way out, even in the Church, on occasion. It goes without saying that the woman experiences traumatic physical, emotional, and spiritual consequences. The horror inflicted often cannot be healed in this life.

The whole situation makes God seem a bit less arbitrary. He didn't establish laws to keep us from having fun. He is the Creator, and He knew when He made the laws that there were laws of spirit and nature already in effect, which, if broken, would cause severe consequences. To help us avoid suffering, He said, "Don't commit adultery." "Flee fornication." He said these things not so He could mock us, but to preserve us for His ultimate calling—a perfect union with a partner and with Him. When we live according to the Manufacturer's recommendations, we last; we live long and prosperous lives.

I've heard it said that fornication is "just a sin of the flesh," and it is. But a fact that we often forget is that we have an enemy who has made it his job to destroy. He goes about in whatever form he must assume to attack our weaknesses. He is a deceiver, making those of us who feel strong think we can handle an occasional relaxing of our standards. He has tricks that lead us down a path of gradual acceptance of wrong. He works on the mind and the obvious frustrations of the single person. A lonely Christian is one of his prime targets, because he knows exactly where the weakness lies.

The weakness may not be sexual at first. The weakness is often loneliness and emptiness. The devil takes hold of the weakness and distorts it, magnifies it, harasses it, and causes us to seek relief from just about any source.

Satan would have us believe that our war is "just" fleshly. But Paul says the warfare is spiritual (see 2 Corinthians 10:3, 4).

Have you ever tried to go into the presence of God in prayer

with your lover? Can you feast on His Word and minister the
fruit of the Spirit after compromising God's will for you?

Of course, you can't, really. You begin to experience guilt,
and Satan heaps on more guilt, convincing you you've gone
too far to pray, so you don't. In walks spiritual sin—and soon
spiritual starvation.

Just a fleshly sin?

Sin is destructive. Not just emotionally, but spiritually, and
sometimes physically.

God's requirements are for our benefit. He knows how He
made us, and what we're able to bear.

God loves us and has provided a way of escape. To the
natural man, it seems unnatural to live without sex. To the
spiritual person, we never have to be subject to "natural"
drives. God's supernatural Spirit within us can perform miracles we don't even understand. He has promised that "There
hath no temptation taken you but such as is common to man:
but God is faithful, who will not suffer you to be tempted
above that ye are able; but will with the temptation also make
a way to escape, that ye may be able to bear it" (1 Corinthians
10:13 KJV). He can take our very natural desires and temporarily set them aside until we can be satisfied within His plan. We
have to want Him to perform that miracle, and He will. There
will be setbacks and flashbacks and perhaps a momentary
stumble. But we have His promise to "keep us from falling."

After all this, I wouldn't have anyone feel condemned.
Rather, like the adulteress in the Gospel, you and your lover
can encounter God, and you will most certainly be led by Him
to ". . . go and sin no more." The Lord had no condemnation for the miserable adulteress, whose humiliation must have
been complete. He said, ". . . Neither do I condemn
thee . . . ." But, in His compassion, He gave her (and many
others) a personal word, ". . . Neither do I condemn thee:
go, and sin no more" (John 8:11 KJV).

As we go on, in this book, talking about the problems that confront singles, I hope that we can all keep in mind the simplicity and the gloriousness that God provides for each of us in this life. Some of the following chapters may be a bit more nitty-gritty than those found in the average Christian book, but in the leading of the Lord, and in my own life experience, I sincerely feel we need to talk about the questions and learn to appropriate the practical answers God has given us.

There is suffering in the world that comes with the world, and there is suffering that is needless. If some of the discussions that follow alleviate, in some way, the needless suffering of single people, we can thank the Lord together.

3
Emotional Monsters

In American society, where personal convenience and pleasure, prosperity and technology abound, we are experiencing in epidemic proportions that severe disorder called "the inferiority complex."

Somewhere along the way, someone came up with the idea of Mr. or Miss Perfect. Artists' conceptions, calendar girls, fashion magazines, motion pictures—all have appointed a standard that says, "This is the ideal." The girls on "Charlie's Angels" are the latest to be upheld as perfection, but most women know they can never look like one of those "angels." Try though we may to copy the latest fashion models, what we usually create are feelings of discontent and self-rejection. And most likely we feel that men reject us because they seek the "ideal," and they feel cheated because they have been stuck with someone who is less than beautiful.

Men don't get by that easily though, because the Six Million Dollar Man, Burt Reynolds, and Robert Redford aren't too bad either. We women also have our dreams of the "macho" one who will be our knight in shining armor. Most men don't live up to the "ideal," and so a frustrating quest for the unattainable propels us into torturous rites of imitation, projection of false images, and concealment of "the real me."

We become rather hard to live with (for ourselves as well as others) when we try so frantically to become something we're not. It's doubly frustrating when we try to change the unchangeable in our appearances.

The problem of inferiority doesn't lie just with personal appearance, but also in achievement and the need to excel. The spirit of competition is perpetuated throughout the educational system and athletic contests. Competition is a healthy motivational factor, but for those who can't be straight-A students, the Homecoming Queen, or Mr. Touchdown, the old "poor me's" take over, and "I can't" turns us all into real underachievers.

The advertising media has also declared that possession of "things" is a sign of status, and they've done a remarkable job of making us believe that our teeth aren't white enough, our car isn't sleek enough, and our hair is the wrong color. The expenditures for these "needs" would be enough to break a John Paul Getty. I guess one very good purpose of capitalism is to create within consumers a sense of need, so we'll buy more, and the free enterprise system flourishes.

I'm glad I live in America and that our system works, but it almost works too well. We see the ads, imagine ourselves to be the chief among the "have nots," and shrink away, believing "I don't have what it takes." We throw a giant "pity party" for ourselves, all alone in our rooms, concentrating on every negative we can conjure up.

If you are single and have read this far, I don't have to describe in any more detail what we do to ourselves in the emotional realm. You already know! I know! In fact, I was an expert hostess for the personal pity parties.

I had a daily routine that was difficult to break. (Singles tend to become set in their ways.) Get up in the morning. Go to work. Come home. Put records on the stereo. Heat the TV dinner. Eat it with the company of a magazine or book, watch TV, go to bed, get up . . . . One evening I noticed that I was beginning to feel terribly depressed and lonely after a relatively good day. "How could this be?" I wondered. I retraced my steps and discovered that I was my own worst enemy.

The music on the stereo could turn the happiest person into a lonely, sexually frustrated crybaby. I sang the tearjerkers right along with Andy Williams and Barbra Streisand. And my reading material wasn't exactly uplifting either. I was stirring up memories of what could never be again, dreaming dreams that could never happen, and, generally speaking, wallowing in the pits of despair.

I then took what I know now to be a major step on my way to self-acceptance and positive living. I said, "I'm tired of being sad." And believe me, I *was*. First of all, away with the "blues" music and on with stimulating and uplifting sounds—mainly gospel music that mysteriously soothes the frayed nerve endings of the soul. (Something like David playing his rejuvenating Psalms for a miserable King Saul.)

Rather than pity parties, I tried my hand at creative outlets that I had never imagined I could do—and I found out I could! Nights alone became valuable time to accomplish fun projects that the working person can't do during the day. This might have something to do with "redeeming the time" and "think on these things" in Ephesians 5 and Philippians 4. It worked and was a beginning on the path that led to an "I can" attitude which began to change my entire life-style.

You can really believe that I took great pains to hide my supposed inferiorities and inadequacies from my friends. I read all the "how to" books, attempting to become what I thought I needed to be to get that special "one" and to be successful at something.

Try as we may to appear carefree and happy, we *know* that deep inside we're lacking, and it eats away at our souls like a cancer. We really believe that there's *no way* we can be what others want us to be, when all the time we are placing requirements on ourselves that may be entirely unnecessary.

Psychologists' couches sag with people who need analysis,

therapy, counseling, and guidance—all in an attempt to become acceptable to themselves.

Granted, some of us do need a major overhaul; it is up to *us* to do some of it. There are some physical changes that need to be made, and we can make them: such as dropping that excess weight and styling our hair in a fashion becoming to the total picture. Fashion magazines and "how to" books are an aid in this area. And we can drop a harsh, offensive demeanor, and just maybe stop being the guest of honor at our own pity parties.

Often when I'm talking with singles about their problems in relating to one another, I ask them this question: "Would you choose *yourself* to be your own roommate?" It takes a moment to understand the question and then a moment to realize that there may be room for some improvements.

When all that can be done on the outside is done, hopefully, with the passage of time and the wisdom of years, we begin to relax and accept ourselves for what we are. We realize that we've made it thus far with small breasts or a big nose or thick ankles; and that people still like us and love us and that we can get a job or run a house. It doesn't matter so much, after all. And that gives us confidence. Then it becomes almost like a chain reaction; if we have confidence in ourselves, others will have confidence in us, too. This changes our relationships with each other and our professional lives—all for the better.

We all have known someone whom we thought of as "perfect" in appearance, and we've quaked in the comparison. But we know, too, that after we've known them for a while, we don't see what they look like anymore; we see what they are. The frantic efforts to become acceptable externally really do nothing to enhance our inner beauty and character which, in the end, form the basis of our acceptance.

While we're crying out for love and acceptance by just one person who will be special to us and who will return the love, we carry the emotional monsters over into our spiritual lives and our acceptance of, and by, God. We assume He's demanding perfection of us and won't love us totally until we've become all we know we're supposed to be. The spiritual inferiority complex sets us back just as much as our emotional insecurities.

We start with comparisons. We look around and say, "If I could just have a ministry like _____." Christendom has created current heroes: great people of God who have public ministries which God is blessing. And, oh, how we *long* to be used of God—to know that we are worthwhile in His Kingdom.

But it seems He's asking so much. There are so many rules and such high standards. We feel no one except the very elite (famous Christians) are able to live up to the Sermon on the Mount. And when Jesus says we are to be *perfect,* we know we're defeated. Rather than attempt to heal the cancer victim or preach a sermon or write a book, we warm a pew on Sunday morning and dutifully drop our tithe into the offering plate, leaving the really important things to the "spiritual giants" who have arrived at some supposedly higher level of spirituality.

Just as I felt the severe pangs of inferiority in my emotional life, I let them cripple me in my spiritual life, too. Gradually, as God thrust me into situations where I had to use the knowledge I had, I discovered I had been given some gifts that were usable within the body of Christ, and I didn't have to wait until I was *perfect* to use them.

Has anyone ever asked you to pray, and you just knew you didn't have the faith to see it answered? Well, I've had that happen to me many times. Outstanding in my memory is an event that occurred shortly after I became Pat Boone's secretary. A nearly hysterical woman telephoned for Pat, and, as usual, he wasn't in the office. Insisting she had to speak to him, the woman began to cry. She told me she had already called the "Prayer Key Family" in Ohio for Rex Humbard, and she couldn't talk to him. She tried to reach Oral Roberts in the Prayer Tower in Oklahoma, and he wasn't there. Now she wanted Pat Boone, and all she got was me.

Crying, she said, "I have to have someone pray for me." With a very smug, pat answer, I said, "We all have the same God, and He can hear you as well as He can hear ministers."

"I can't pray," she said. "God doesn't hear me." She explained that her teenaged son had just taken an overdose of LSD and walked through their plate-glass window. She didn't know what was going to happen next, and she was desperate and frightened.

And then I knew. There had been times I felt I couldn't pray and was just sure my prayers went no higher than the ceiling. So I said, "Would you like for me to pray?" Quickly she said, "Yes, please!" But I didn't mean to pray that moment, over the telephone. I planned on saying a silent prayer when we hung up, or thought I would put in a prayer request at church. She wanted prayer *now*.

I had to. There wasn't anybody else. So I did.

I don't remember what I said. It was a far cry from Oral Roberts or Rex Humbard, but I talked to God. And He heard me! The lady stopped crying, and suddenly there was a "peace that passed all understanding" on her end of the line. I don't know what happened to her son, but I know that God quieted her nerves, and she was able to cope with the situation.

Isn't it sad that God has to force us to try our wings before we learn that we have an important part in the body?

It was a long and sometimes painful learning journey, but He set me on the path, and I'm still trudging along.

Part of that trudging brought me to the position of "teacher" of a singles' Sunday-school class. I didn't think I could do it, but the pastor convinced me I should try, and since there were only about twelve in the class, I decided I could handle it. Within a few months there were thirty, and then forty, and then nearly one hundred. I was scared to death, but since I had made it through each week, I concluded I could make it through the next one, too.

I had a good time teaching the "Single Saints" and found myself putting into my teaching so many of the truths I had been taught at home, in church, and Bible college.

While teaching a study on the Book of Hebrews, I became slightly confused and troubled over the number of times *perfect* was used by the author in relation to God's expectations of people. We are to "go on to *perfection.*" He is the "perfector of our faith." He makes us "perfect in every good work . . . ."

Cross-references direct us to Matthew 5:48, where Jesus says, "Be ye therefore perfect . . ." (KJV). And Paul, throughout his epistles, admonishes Christians to be *perfect.* "Till we all come . . . unto a perfect man . . ." (Ephesians 4:13, KJV).

I began to wonder if God is laying a requirement on us that we can't possibly attain.

In Sunday school, every time I heard anyone talk on those particular commands, he invariably said, "Of course, *nobody is perfect,* but we must have a goal." At the same time, I was told we could never reach that goal in this life, because only Jesus is perfect, and someday when we see Him, we'll be like Him.

I had a hard time accepting that doctrine. I just couldn't believe that God would ask something of us that He knew we couldn't attain. Does He call us to the impossible?

No, not a just God!

What does He mean, then? Or do I labor under the depression of spiritual inferiority, too?

Thank God for Bible commentaries. I don't read Greek, so I read what the scholars say about it. We're faced with the problem of an inadequate language. English translations of the Greek word for *perfect,* which is *teleios,* really don't mean "without fault" or "flawless," as we would suppose. It doesn't mean that God is requiring that we live in a constant state of perfection, always flawlessly manifesting the fruit of the Spirit.

When I read Hebrews 13:20, 21 in the New American Standard Version, I developed a more "perfect" understanding of what God is telling us about ourselves. He says:

> Now the God of peace, who brought up from the dead the great Shepherd of the sheep through the blood of the eternal covenant, even Jesus our Lord, *equip* you in every good thing to do His will, working in us that which is pleasing in His sight, through Jesus Christ, to whom be the glory for ever and ever. Amen. (*Italics added.*)

"The God of peace . . . *equip* you in every good thing to do His will . . . ." The King James Version says "Make you *perfect* . . . to do his will . . ." (*italics added*).

In other words, we are already able and equipped to do something worthwhile in His body.

Second Timothy 3:17 says, "that the man of God may be adequate, *equipped* for every good work" (NAS, *italics added*).

That gives it a different ring. God, then, is simply telling us that He has already equipped us to do His will.

All the time we thought we weren't "spiritual" enough or that we had to "get our act together" before He could use us, and He's saying that we are already perfect for the job He has called us to do.

You've heard the expression "She's just *perfect* for the job." I think that's what God is saying to you. "You're okay the way you are. You don't have to change for Me to accept you. I can use you the way you are: insecure, immature, less than flawless." Not that changes don't need to be made in your life, but you are acceptable and lovable, and He is in the process of taking you from where you are to where you are supposed to

be. As long as you're on the way, you can be used by Him.
What has He called us to do?

People say to me, "Janet, I could never talk in front of
people. I'm not a singer. I can't be a teacher. I don't have
profound wisdom like the pastor." And I say, "Good. We
don't need a church full of pastors and singers and teachers."

Maybe He didn't call you to be a soloist or a teacher or a
pastor.

We tend to glamorize the "spiritual gifts" that are listed in 1
Corinthians, the twelfth through the fourteenth chapters. We
think we have to *do* something spectacular to be "spiritual."
Since we don't "feel" spectacular, we withdraw and suffer the
same kinds of depression, aloneness, and inferiority that
plague us in other personal areas of our lives.

Maybe you are one who has been sitting around saying, "I
am of no value to God. I can't do anything."

Romans, the twelfth chapter, says you can "serve." You can
"give." You can "show mercy with cheerfulness." Read it.
There is something for you to do.

I have a dear friend whose newborn baby had severe birth
defects and extreme retardation. The shock and despair to her
and her husband were beyond most people's comprehension.
Many in the church ministered to them in beautiful ways, and
they were comforted and sustained through the first weeks of
testing and uncertainty. She later told me of the most meaningful gesture of comfort she received. One brother in their
couples' fellowship came to see them. He didn't really know
what to say, and he blurted out some words about being sorry
and wanting to do what he could. Feeling helpless, he just took
her in his arms and cried tears of deep compassion and sorrow.
She hadn't known anyone cared that much, and it released in
her those dammed-up fears and tears and agonies. They cried
together.

"Rejoice with those who rejoice, weep with those who
weep" (Romans 12:15 RSV).

We all know how to cry!

There really is no excuse. You are equipped to get His job done. Start where you are and do what you can do. Grow with the job and become all you are meant to be.

Jesus is coming for a body that is fitly joined and held together by that which every joint supplies, according to the *proper* working of each individual part, causing the growth of the body for the building up of itself in love (*see* Ephesians 4:16).

The beautiful part of Hebrews 13:21 that we often overlook is the assurance that Jesus is ". . . working in us that which is pleasing in His sight . . ." (NAS). If you think you are facing the impossible, don't believe it. He wouldn't ask you to do it if He didn't see you as "perfect for the job."

He never calls us to something that He doesn't also equip us to do.

What more can we ask? He has called us, equipped us, and is working *in* us to do His good pleasure (*see* Philippians 2:13).

This takes us right back to our preoccupation with our appearances, our self-rejection, and our insecurities. The same spiritual principle is applicable in our emotional inferiorities. It isn't self-rejection that propels us to achieve (or withdraw), but acceptance of His acceptance that enables us to advance to maturity, both spiritually and emotionally.

It is not a matter of value and worth, of one person being more important than another. We tend to belittle our "small" gifts and think that spectacular, public ministries are a sign of maturity. I really believe that maturity is nothing more than obedience to *be* all He has called you to be.

He made you the way you are physically, spiritually, and emotionally, and if you want it, He'll give you the desire and the will to see yourself as He sees you—*perfect!*

4

The Broken Heart— Care and Repair

There are all sorts of heart diseases, but among the most common and the most serious is the infamous "broken heart." Among people who have loved, it is a familiar disability.

Colleen Townsend Evans, in her book *Love Is an Everyday Thing,* tells of a woman who actually died in her grief, because her husband had been too shortsighted to forgive her immaturity, and he left her. It has been said that the great American folk-song writer, Stephen Foster, died of a broken heart. Just about everyone has suffered from this painful heart condition. Some are able to recover, but others just can't seem to get over it.

There are no pills for broken hearts. Most people confront the problem with preventive medicine; the human nature within each of us continues to protect and defend the vulnerable places of our human hearts.

We take a multiplicity of routes to escape the disappointment and betrayed trust. Sometimes our efforts to dig our ways out really put us in deeper, and we end up nearly buried alive, intensifying the pain rather than relieving it. Very naturally, almost without conscious forethought, we erect emotional walls of protection, refusing to love or trust anyone. We attempt to harden ourselves, and we lash back with bitterness, hoping vengeance will bring some sort of relief. It doesn't, but there is a certain sadistic satisfaction in thinking we somehow have gotten even. A miserable lot of scorekeepers we become.

Another common route of escape is the busyness that somehow keeps us so active that we don't have time for feelings. We become involved in noble projects: Bible studies, church work, and the like. Singles are notorious for being on "an eternal search," going from singles' group to singles' group, seeking out some unidentified satisfaction. Singles' clubs and computer dating services are doing a land-office business. Uppers and downers—pills to substitute for that nonexistent broken-heart pill—are in high demand among singles. While it might be possible to achieve a "high" by any number of diversions—fast living, busy Christian work, drugs, or booze—we know if there's a "high," there has to be a "low" also, and we're right back where we started, or worse.

But realistically, all activities have to come to an end, and we all must come back to ourselves for a "me, myself, and I" confrontation. That can be rough when all of our activities have been designed to avoid being alone with the hurts.

And, oh, how we relive the events that caused the pain. We go over every detail, wondering what we could have done or said to have prevented the problem. We talk about it, pray about it, and dream about it. But there's no way our human understanding can undo what's been done and heal a broken heart.

We become convinced that we could solve everything with just one more chance. We want to talk over some painful situation just once more from the top. But as much as we plan those hypothetical conversations and go over perfect scripts in our minds, it all amounts to private medicine for a private illness. Somehow, the other party doesn't appreciate the script we wrote, and such efforts are inevitably doomed to failure.

Of course, we suppose that some person or circumstance is

utterly responsible for our broken hearts, and the blame we place actually increases our sadness. The intense concentration on the external situation that caused the painful self-examining in the first place makes the heart become the central focus of our emotions. Sometimes every waking thought becomes forced into the context of that temporarily broken heart. Our perspective on life becomes distorted.

Perspective is a funny thing. When I was a child, I just detested the afternoon naps I had to take. I would lie in bed talking to myself, playing, and doing anything I could to keep myself from going to sleep. One day, while lying on my bed, looking at the lines and cracks in the ceiling, I raised my arm and looked down it to my hand, using my index finger as a sight, much as one would look down a rifle barrel at the sight. As I played this little game, I was startled to find that my finger and hand were larger than the ceiling. I knew that in reality my hand was dwarfed when compared to the size of the room; but when I used my hand as a pointer, with my viewpoint from behind my hand, it became larger than life, and my room was nothing but a hazy blur. When my surroundings were viewed with my hand away from my eyes, the room was its normal size, and everything was in focus. This was a fun diversion for a child who didn't want to go to sleep.

But it's not very much fun for an adult playing that game with life's circumstances. When I became older and had experienced more of life and love and pain, I found myself thinking a lot about the unpleasant experiences I'd had. I asked a lot of "why" questions of God and tried to undo some of the mistakes. I prayed a lot for better things to happen. I contrived ways to manipulate "fate" and prayed some more that God would undo the damage and make everything right again. But I continued to suffer from the constant hurt that was aroused by the memories I was always focusing on.

And finally it occurred to me that I was viewing life's situations in much the same manner I had viewed the cracks in the ceiling of my bedroom many years ago. No wonder I was so sad! No wonder all of life seemed to be an endurance test, and I could see no light at the end of the tunnel. I was concentrating so vigorously on the pain and emotional problems that the rest of life was out of focus. I was magnifying my problems in the way I had magnified my index finger. My problems seemed bigger than all of the rest of life. My viewpoint always tainted the thing I said I was trying to forget, and I didn't forget it. I continued to harass myself with memories.

This revelation woke me up, and I decided that I was tired of being sad. I took stock of myself, and found I had been doing all the right things on the surface, but deep inside I was still nurturing my wounds. I was busy in church and lots of activities, but they were only temporary escapes from reality. It seemed that I had become my own worst enemy by deliberately prolonging my suffering. Now I wanted out. I wanted to change my focal point, and I began to search for a way to heal the fragmented ends of my emotions and nerves and inner spirit.

Where could I go, though, for the answer? I thought I *knew* all the answers. I'd been brought up in church, taught Bible classes, and attended Bible college. But there must be something more!

I had been taught that Jesus loved me, but it had been difficult to personalize "me." I really believed that "Jesus loved the children of the world." I imagined that He had corralled them all into one giant arena and loved them collectively; you know, all the children sitting in the Sunday-school classroom had His love, but not *me*. But now I wanted to know if my religion was doing anything for me, or if I was in it because I was brainwashed. If Jesus did love me, then I had to get to know Him differently than I ever had before.

At that time in my life, I was living in a small town, recuperating from a genuine breakdown and some very traumatic personal events in my life. For several months, I had nothing to do but read the Bible; I had no phone, no television, and very little to do socially. There was no Bible bookstore for books or tapes—just me, the Holy Spirit, and the Word.

I desperately needed to know Jesus. I needed to know what He is *really* like. The Jesus I had read about in textbooks and heard about in children's Sunday-school stories just didn't seem to be adequate for my needs. If Jesus was who He said He was, then my needs should have been met, and I shouldn't have been in the predicament I found myself in. So, I read the Gospels to find out what Jesus would do *now* if He were right here with me. I thought about what He would say to me if I could sit down for a cup of coffee with Him or go for a walk. As I read about His life, I took note of what He said and did each time He met someone personally, and I found that He always met him at the point of his need when the chips were down.

I came to Luke 4:18, where Jesus read from Isaiah 61, which says:

> The Spirit of the Lord God is upon me; because the Lord hath anointed me to preach good tidings unto the meek; he hath sent me to bind up the brokenhearted, to proclaim liberty to the captives, and the opening of the prison to them that are bound; To proclaim the acceptable year of the Lord, and the day of vengeance of our God; to comfort all that mourn; To appoint unto them that mourn in Zion, to give unto them beauty for ashes, the oil of joy for mourning, the garment of praise for the spirit of heaviness; that they might be called trees of righteousness, the planting of the Lord, that he might be glorified.
>
> Isaiah 61:1–3 KJV

That was quite a breakthrough for me. I don't know where I'd been each time I'd read those verses before, but all of a

sudden I got the idea that Jesus was more concerned about
me than He was with my keeping the rules and busying myself
with church activities. For me, a ray of hope shone through the
long tunnel of despair.

But I was skeptical. I wondered, "Can I be totally healed of
something that's so deep?" I doubted it. However, I was so
desperate that finding out was worth the chance. The Holy
Spirit caused me to search and read and meditate, and I
learned that Jesus is intimately concerned and can and will
fulfill that prophecy in Isaiah 61 if we want Him to.

I wanted Him to. And I asked Him to.

The reality of what God can do in a life came to me as I was
walking down the street in my little town one afternoon. My
town was Elko, Nevada, and it had a cowboys-and-Indians
problem. Elko is a western cowboy town that looks as if it
could be a movie set for a turn-of-the-century western—with
the exception of automobiles and TV antennas. Elko has cow-
boys and Indians, and they still get into fights.

The Indians were treated horribly, and I found their condi-
tions despicable. In truth, I was a little afraid of them, and I
avoided them as much as I could. I just didn't want to go near
them. My job as a bookkeeper for a law firm required that I go
to the bank every day. The short two-block walk could take me
past the local Indian bar, or I could cross the street to avoid
them. I'd heard stories about Indians when they got drunk,
and I didn't want to take any chances, so I always crossed the
street.

But one day, as I was walking, thinking about Jesus and
asking Him about my life and what was to come, I came
face-to-face with a young Indian couple walking toward me,
with a child between them, holding hands and laughing. I saw
that this was a happy family, and I realized that those men I
found so disgusting were once laughing little boys like that
child. As I rounded the corner and began to cross the street to
avoid the Indian crowd, as usual, I stopped short. "I bet Jesus

wouldn't cross the street," I thought. And suddenly I knew what Jesus would do if He walked those streets today: He would walk among them and reach out to them, saying, "Be whole, be whole."

And I wanted to walk among them and reach out, saying, "Yes, be whole. Jesus makes us whole." I didn't do it because I was afraid nothing would happen, but it was a turning point in my life and in my understanding of Jesus. Luke 4:18 took on a new meaning: Jesus cares, and He came to make me whole, not just spiritual.

He came to set me free from the terrible emotions that bound me in a self-made prison that was worse than the cells of a dungeon. He came to give me the option of exchanging my mourning for His oil of joy, to give me beauty for the ashes of my pride, and to give me the garment of praise instead of the spirit of heaviness, that I might be called "a tree of righteousness."

My new awareness of the ministry of Jesus started a new awareness of His healing of my broken heart. I made a new commitment. I said, "Lord, this is the Jesus I want to minister to the world."

All of my searching and crying and manipulation did not heal me, but my awareness of Jesus the Healer was the beginning. He requires our cooperation and submission and our trust that He does all things well. I had begun a journey and felt as if I couldn't get to my destination fast enough. More study of Jesus' teachings gave me some clear instructions about how I was to behave toward those who despitefully used me and hurt me. Though Jesus is the Healer, there were some very specific things I had to do, too.

He said we're to love them and forgive them and pray for them.

Being the human creatures that we are, we say, "Yes, but You don't know what happened . . . ." Jesus also said we can do anything He did and greater things; and because He forgave, it is possible for us to love and forgive those who have hurt us.

In fact, He said, if you're about to present yourself at the altar and remember that your brother has something against you, you'd better leave your offering there and go be reconciled to him and then come back to present your offering (*see* Matthew 5:23, 24). He also said, "But if you do not forgive men, then your Father will not forgive your transgressions" (Matthew 6:15 RSV). He taught so beautifully in His model prayer that we are asking God to "forgive our trespasses as [in the same way] we forgive those who trespass against us."

But, if He forgives us the way we actually forgive others, we may not get much forgiveness! Could that be one of the reasons for my prolonged suffering? My intense concentration on the hurt blinded me to the possibility that forgiveness can sever that negative emotional tie I had with that to which I was bound. Spiritual surgery takes place at the time of forgiveness, cuts the negative tie that binds, and brings about the freedom we so desperately want.

If forgiveness is what we are required to do, how do we do it? Did Jesus really suffer the same things we suffer? Was He that human, or did He still have enough of His God-ness in Him to make Him something different from what we are?

Philippians 2 says that He became equal with man, taking on the form of a lowly person. Hebrews says He was tempted in all parts just as we are. He grew tired, He was hungry, He wept. Yes, I believe He was human, and He knew it wasn't easy to forgive! He also knew that forgiveness is the only way to freedom.

Talk about rejection and hurt! Jesus lived with it daily. His own hometown wouldn't receive Him, and He had to leave there without performing any miracles, because they didn't have faith. That hurt!

Then there were all those temple leaders who were so knowledgeable in the Scriptures and taught all the classes and performed all the rites. They should have been the very ones to receive Him with love. But they felt threatened and couldn't give up their acts of self-righteousness or prestigious man-made positions to accept His simple teachings of love and humility and forgiveness. These were His people, His own race, the people God sent Him to redeem.

Certain ones among Jesus' people had the humility to accept Him and obtain salvation through Him. They went on with His works, and they built the Christian church. But, as for the leaders, they had Him thrown out of the temple, and He had to escape for His life. They talked about Him consorting with publicans and sinners and questionable women. When they couldn't stop Him, they had Him killed.

Human nature has us wait for our enemies to ask for our forgiveness. But the ones who killed Jesus didn't ask, and He forgave them anyway! Even while He was suffering such agony, He asked His Father to forgive them because they didn't know what they were doing.

But those were His enemies! We can't really expect to be overwhelmed with good from our enemies, can we? What about our family and friends who inflict pain?

Wait a minute; we don't get off that easily. Jesus' *friends* weren't much better some of the time.

Remember when He was really in a troubled state of mind, just before His enemies dragged Him away to be crucified? He already knew Judas was going to betray Him, and He knew it was going to be the most difficult moment He would ever have to face. He tried to communicate this to His closest friends, the disciples, and asked them to come pray with Him. They went to their favorite spot, and He stationed a few of them and walked on with the three who seemed to be closer to Him than the rest: Peter, James, and John. He just asked them to watch and pray with Him for one hour—to help Him get through this bitter ordeal that was to come upon Him.

Just an hour, and when He returned to them, His three

closest friends were asleep. They all scattered when He was arrested, and one of them even denied that he'd ever known Him.

Talk about being disappointed by your Christian friends! Jesus was going through pain and needed all the support and strength He could get, and they couldn't even stay awake, because they just didn't understand what He had tried to share with them.

Yes, He knows all about our hurts. He knows about the insensitivities of people and misunderstandings of close friends and family. He also knew that carrying grudges of hate, bitterness, and resentment is the same as nurturing a festering sore. Our grudges become inflamed each time we think about the problems or persons who have inflicted the pain. The negative emotions we resurrect actually become the central focus of our beings, and bind us to the problems rather than offering the solutions.

Jesus knew that forgiveness, in God's beautiful and mystical way, frees us from our burdens of hate and at the same time releases the other people from our emotional grasps. As we're released from these emotions, our grips loosen, and we're set free from those hateful things that were binding us into lives of misery.

I know it's difficult to believe that our forgiveness will heal the broken hearts that are binding us. Often we don't "feel" free, or we think we can't honestly forgive. We may say the words, but still feel the bondage.

We all know that feelings don't guarantee anything; God's Word does. And He said, "For if you forgive men their trespasses, your heavenly Father also will forgive you" (Matthew 6:14 RSV). So, forgive others and ask the Father to forgive you (*see* 1 John 1:9). Ask Him to forgive them, too! Believe that the healing process is in motion. God will carry out His end of the deal if we carry out ours. In fact, He'll go the extra mile. He'll perform the miracles to heal the memories as well as the wounds; He puts our pieces back together and makes us whole.

Forgiveness is a fact, not a feeling. Forgiveness does, indeed, begin the healing process, and those negative emotional ties are cut. But we must be careful not to become entangled in them again. Jesus taught another marvelous principle here—pray! Yes, Jesus said to pray for our enemies and those who despitefully use us. That's not just a nice, holy-sounding platitude; it's a spiritual law that, when followed, has a tremendous effect. You just can't hate someone very long if you pray for them.

I don't mean to pray that he (or she) will return to your loving embrace or that he'll make proper amends or receive his just punishment. Just pray that he'll experience God's love in His fullness, and let God take care of the details of each situation. If restitution is in order, do it joyfully and freely.

Bask in the love of Jesus and let the healing oil of His Spirit soothe the wounds with joy instead of mourning. Exchange your spirit of heaviness for the garment of praise and become a tree of righteousness, firmly planted by the Lord, glorifying Him.

And see if that doesn't repair your broken heart.

5

Love—What God Is, and Other Definitions

"What is this thing called love?"

I talk to single people all the time who want to be loved. Recently, a couple of gals in their early thirties cried out to me something on the order of the following:

"What is love? Where is it?"

"I hate people. No, I don't; I want people to like me."

"I just want someone to love me."

In fact, if you could read the mail I read every day, and answer our phones, you'd see that those jumbled feelings are very common, and that's really a sad commentary on our society. So many people are dying slow deaths for lack of love, and I'm grieved because I know that love is so close to them, and yet so far.

Whatever love is, it's the greatest power in the universe. Songs have been written about it, thrones have been abandoned for it, wars have been fought for it, and men and women have died for it. Yet love is almost undefinable, because it can't be discerned with any of the five senses. Some times when you have love, you don't know it; and some times when you think you have it, you find out it's not the real thing at all.

Surely love has to be more than a feeling and more than a fleeting sexual experience.

I've read that the English language is not the best language on earth for adequate expression, and I believe it! Take the word *love,* for example. People say, "I love pizza." "I love baseball." "I love children." "I love animals." How can one possibly use the same word to describe feelings for pizza and for a person? Is one's love of animals the same as one's love of sports? I think not! There is a good feeling and attraction for each of these things, but our feelings for each one are different. Perhaps it would be more accurate to say that the things we "love" seem good to us because of the way they make us feel. If something makes us feel good, naturally we want to be around it or have it with us as often as possible. But our desire to eat pizza as often as possible is very unlike our desire to be with our friends as often as possible. Yet, we want them both. So what are we going to do with the word *love?* We're using *love* to cover everything, but that just doesn't adequately express our true feelings.

In the Greek language, there are three words for love: first is *agape* (perfect), then *phileo* (brotherly), and then *eros* (sensual).

Let's begin with *eros,* because it is the one kind of love we all know something about. Eros was the Greek god of love, equivalent to the Roman god Cupid. Cupid is familiar to all of us, with his cute little wings and bow and arrows.

According to Dr. Theodor Bovet, a Swiss physician and marriage counselor, Cupid didn't just aim his arrows at the sex drive of the body; he aimed at the heart. Doctor Bovet says:

> Eros does all it can to bring out the specifically masculine or feminine characteristics of the personality. Grace and kindness, charm and delicacy on the one side; chivalry, courage, gentlemanly behavior and attentiveness on the other; all these are, in the best sense of the word, erotic things . . . . Eros . . . gives pleasure to both partners at the same time,

enables them to give themselves to each other, entering into each other, stilling their own egos for the sake of each other.

The current definition of *eros* has degraded it to gratification of biological passions, with no concern for the satisfaction of the other person involved. This shows how far we've digressed from the real thing.

Everyone has sexual drives that require satisfaction, and that's normal. But unfortunately, somewhere along the line we confused *eros* (sexual satisfaction) with true love. When *eros* is experienced for only what we can get out of it, then it's not love at all, unless we're honest and call it "love of self." Often in our search for true love, we dehumanize ourselves by becoming objects of *eros* (sex). That infamous concept, "Love American Style," is nothing more than a few moments of sensual pleasure that quickly ends and then requires more pursuit and more eroticism from just about any source. There are people who act as if they don't know anything else.

Then there's the *phileo* kind of love. We get *Philadelphia*, the "City of Brotherly Love," from *phileo*. And that's what *phileo* is: brotherly love. Brotherly love is good, and we need it. A lot of philanthropic people are doing fine things in the world because of this kind of love. It is a feeling of goodwill toward mankind. *Phileo* is "one human being drawn to another and relating with affection and fondness." But *phileo* is as unpredictable as the human being expressing it. It is generally based on the performance of the person being loved. I've heard *phileo* described this way: "I'll love you, but don't cross me." Or, "I'll scratch your back if you'll scratch mine."

If our lives are going well, then our expression of *phileo* is fairly consistent. But let a few bad breaks come along, and *phileo* becomes insecure and full of mistrust, jealousy, hate, criticism, anger, and so on. Consequently, *phileo* can't really be trusted completely, because it comes from the human level of understanding, and therefore, at best, is temporary and inconsistent.

We all experience times when we are not very lovable, and the *phileo* someone has for us quickly fades into what we see as rejection. And when the *phileo* fails, and the *eros* has dehumanized us, what is left?

More than erotic love and unpredictable *phileo: agape!*

In this era of the "Jesus Movement," singing groups call themselves *"Agape."* There are orphanages and halfway houses called *"Agape."* Sermons are being preached and songs are being sung about *agape.* It has become such an overused word that it's a wonder we really understand true *agape* love.

Real *agape* says, "I'll love you even if you walk on me." *Agape* says, "You can stone me, falsely accuse me, drag me through the streets, ridicule me. You can give me a mock trial and fake coronation and robe and crown, and I'll forgive you and love you anyway."

Agape is patient and kind, never jealous or envious, never boastful or proud, never haughty or selfish or rude. *Agape* does not demand its own way. It is not irritable or touchy. It does not hold grudges and will hardly ever notice when others do it wrong. It is never glad about injustice, but rejoices whenever truth wins out. If you love someone with *agape,* you will be loyal to him, no matter what the cost. You will always believe in him, always assume the best of him, and always stand your ground in defending him (*see* 1 Corinthians 13:4–7).

With the above definition in mind, when you say, "I love sports," you would hardly mean "I *agape* sports." Nor would you mean "I *agape* pizza," or whatever the object of your attraction. In fact, it really is difficult to truly *agape* anything or anyone.

We use the word *love* too frequently, and consequently, in our quest for the feeling of being loved and loving, we get these three loves all mixed up. A person having sex with someone—total strangers or married lovers—can say the words "I love you," and somehow they'll both hear "I *agape* you," when what is really meant is, "I love the sensation this act is giving me." There's something mysterious about the sex act that for a brief moment makes one feel really wanted, so people fool themselves into thinking they're always important to their sex partner. Since *eros* (sexual love) lasts about as long as the sexual experience, it's easy for a person to become addicted to sex in an effort to hang on to that fleeting moment of belonging. This honest search for love is an easy way to justify illicit sex, all because "I just want to be loved."

Most of us, at one time or another, really did love someone and thought we were loved in return. We counted on that person's love to live up to our expectations of pure *agape*. All of our hopes and desires were wrapped up in the person or persons we loved. But when the *agape* proved to be fickle *phileo* and/or *eros*, the deep wounds inflicted upon our innermost beings almost destroyed us. We try to figure out what we did wrong, convince ourselves that we're just not "lovable," and experience a painful sense of rejection. We become resentful, and our self-worth plummets to the depths of despair. We assume a phony behavior pattern that belies what's really inside.

After a few experiences of being hurt, we're not about to deliberately ask for more. We attempt to withdraw from any expression of love and refuse to express what we really feel, because loving is too dangerous. Life becomes an unpleasant guessing game of "he loves me; he loves me not." We hide behind walls of emotional protection and determine to take no more risks. With cosmetic exteriors and bleeding interiors, we hope nothing can penetrate our walls. Unfortunately, behind our calloused walls are the same sensitive selves that are longing for *agape* love.

Most of us admit that we need people, and that's true. We all do. But how can we live in a close, trusting relationship with someone when our understanding of love is so confused?

As I see it, one of the problems is that we put too much hope in a person or persons.

Remember, the natural cry of our hearts is to be loved and accepted. People have tried to find this in just about every possible way—from relationships, to drugs, to role playing, to church—you know where you've looked for something to satisfy that deep inner longing for love.

But do you think that only a person—a human being—can give you what you need? Well, God knows if that is true, and it's up to God, not people, to see that all our needs are met. He has ways of accomplishing everything that must be done— even meeting all our needs. If the person you're counting on fails to live up to God's requirements, *God will see to it that your needs are supplied.* Believe that, because God says it and does it!

Many times, our own negative reactions to the people who have hurt us are the very things we are complaining about in other people. It turns out that we've been requiring something from someone that we are incapable of giving, and that is pure, unadulterated *agape.*

In the church, we've been taught that we're supposed to act and be like Jesus. We try to be, and we can't; and we want it from others, and *they* can't. We pray that God will give us what we need, and it turns out that what we need is what we're supposed to *be* (like Jesus). Sounds like an unending circle.

The very kind of love needed—love that will never fail, never criticize; love that will accept us along with our faults and understand us if we fail—is *agape.* Wouldn't it be great to have someone whose shoulder we could cry on and who could give us *agape* love? Even behind the thick walls we've erected, we still have to cope with our need for that kind of understanding. The irony of the whole thing is that the very One we tend to blame for all our misery is the only One who can give the agape we must have.

You know who I mean—God!

God?

I can almost hear you saying, "I want someone who will touch and see and hear me, even when I'm unattractive and unlovable." For sure, that's what we all need, and that's what God actually offers. But we're putting the cart before the horse. We want *phileo* mixed with *eros* and *agape,* but *agape* must come first. Pure *agape*—not from a human, but from Love Himself.

First John, the fourth chapter, says, "God *is* love." Not that He has some love to give us, but He *is* love! Not that He'll love you if you perform by the rules, but He *is* love! His love is not conditional. His love cannot reject. By virtue of His very nature, His love is perfect love (*see* 1 Corinthians 13).

Okay, there's still that vacuum inside us that requires *agape* (God). The problem starts when we try to fill the vacuum with *phileo* and/or *eros* (imperfect love) from humans. It doesn't satisfy, and we'll never be satisfied until we fill that hole with the only love that we were created for: God's *agape* love.

How do you fill the emptiness? The woman at the well seemed to be craving fulfillment. She'd even tried five husbands and at least one man who wasn't her husband. Nicodemus had kept the rules since his birth and had gone to all the services at the temple and was an upstanding citizen, and yet he knew something was missing from his life. Zacchaeus, the man who sought fulfillment through material goods, grabbed at everyone's money for his solution, and that failed, too.

Jesus told them all, "Receive Me." Fill that vacancy with God's Spirit—*agape.* Begin at the beginning, new birth, and you'll receive all the other things you need.

The craving of our spirits, which we can only identify as an emptiness that must be filled with some kind of love, is invariably satisfied with God's love. We must be filled with His love and ask the Father to give us the Holy Spirit. Jesus promised that to us in Luke 11:13. He will fill our inner beings with rivers of living water, which causes a constant quenching of the longing we've had.

Phileo and *eros* will naturally follow in proper sequence and priority. You will still have the need for affection and sensual satisfaction, but that burning drive to satisfy yourself (and protect yourself) won't be there. Circumstances may not change, but you will be changed. Instead of having a vacuum inside, you will have the sense of well-being you've always wanted: love, joy, peace, patience, kindness, understanding, and so on. When people come down hard on you, you'll understand that they could act no differently than they did, because perhaps they didn't know the meaning of real love, either. They thought love was conditional, and they, too, were probably defending some sensitive spot in themselves. Human love doesn't know what else to do.

The more you get to know God and His love, the more you will learn to let His love come out through your personality. And when His love comes through you, people around you begin to change. Love *requires* change!

The changes may come slowly, and you may have setbacks, but as you learn to identify God's love inside you and experience Him, your step-by-step daily life will take on a new focus and meaning. You'll develop a better understanding, and you'll respond with love as you would have people love you.

Listen to what God is saying to us all about how to love:

> Dear friends, let us practice loving each other, for love comes from God and those who are loving and kind show that they are the children of God, and that they are getting to know him better. But if a person isn't loving and kind, it shows that he doesn't know God—for God is love. God showed how much he

loved us by sending his only Son into this wicked world to bring to us eternal life through his death. In this act we see what real love is: it is not our love for God, but his love for us when he sent his Son to satisfy God's anger against our sins. Dear friends, since God loved us as much as that, we surely ought to love each other too. For though we have never yet seen God, when we love each other God lives in us and his love within us grows ever stronger.

1 John 4:7–12 LB

Does *eros* fit into all of this?

When you have experienced God's love, your *phileo* relationships with people will be based upon completely different standards, and you won't demand something they can't give. In the same way, you can see the difference between gratification of the body and acceptance of your whole being. You no longer have to give your body for a moment of belonging. When you find someone to whom you can express *agape* and *phileo* in their highest forms, perhaps this is the one that God has for your expression of perfect *eros*. *Eros,* without the sanctification of God, will only bring that same frustration which people are trying to escape. But *eros* through the eyes of *agape* is sanctioned by God's holy covenant, binding two individuals together in His *agape*. What a beautiful threefold love experience—with lifetime satisfaction guaranteed!

It took me a very long time to say, "God loves you!"

We know how much God loves us because we have felt his love and because we believe him when he tells us that he loves us dearly. God is love, and anyone who lives in love is living with God and God is living in him. And as we live with Christ, our love grows more perfect and complete; so we will not be ashamed and embarrassed at the day of judgment, but can face him with confidence and joy, because he loves us and we love him too. We need have no fear of someone who loves us perfectly; his perfect love for us eliminates all dread of what he might do to us. If we are afraid, it is for fear of what he might do to us, and shows that we are not fully convinced that he really loves us.

1 John 4:16–18 LB

In other words, don't be afraid. God won't allow anything to come your way that you can't handle. He will give you everything that is good for you, and He'll lead you gently and securely into a position of self-confidence, self-worth, and self-love—*agape* love.

Yes, you can be filled with His *agape* love; it's there just for you to willfully and consciously accept. You don't have to have a big, emotional experience, just the calm acceptance of His promise that He is your loving Father and will provide everything you need.

Accept other people for what they are: imperfect people who may not know God's love. Accept fellow Christians as nonperfected people who have experienced God's love but are showing it imperfectly. Accept *yourself* as a person who wants God's love but doesn't as yet know how to let it become all of his life.

Don't worry about anything; instead, pray about everything; tell God your needs and don't forget to thank him for his answers. If you do this you will experience God's peace, which is far more wonderful than the human mind can understand. His peace will keep your thoughts and your hearts quiet and at rest as you trust in Christ Jesus.

Philippians 4:6, 7 LB

6
Masturbation and Its Troubles

There is a certain problem a lot of people are trying to deal with and very few people are willing to discuss—particularly in the Christian church.

There have been taboos on this act for centuries, it seems, and it has been cloaked with an air of suspicion and perversion. Every form of abnormalcy from crossed eyes to insanity has been attributed to it, and somehow, even though it is barely mentioned by most parents, children have a built-in sense of shame and guilt if they engage in this form of self-play and gratification. Grown-up children take this same guilt and fear along with them into adulthood.

But what about this thing we call masturbation, that is spoken of in whispers? Does God have anything to say about it in His Book?

My own investigation and the study of respected Christian scholars and psychologists can find nothing in the entire Bible relating to this subject. It is apparent, in studying God's Word, that He is very thorough, and He is capable of letting us know in no uncertain terms what is sin and what is not. He has unconditionally specified that certain things are sin, and He has stated that there is chastisement due to anyone who breaks His laws.

Does it seem strange that something that for centuries has caused intense guilt and controversy (and even imprisonment) is not even mentioned in the Bible? Could it be that man has called something unclean that God has *not* called unclean? If so, man has placed a burden of sin and guilt upon himself that God did not intend him to bear.

A few Christians, in an attempt to be open and non-judgmental, have made good strides in trying to relieve people of this guilt. But with this attempt they also suggest that in order to have a healthy mind and body and to prevent the dangers of living in fantasy and obsession, don't do it. It's sort of like the old adage, "Where there's doubt—don't!"

I'm not going to give an endorsement of masturbation. In fact, I think the principle Jesus used with the disciples and Pharisees in Matthew 19 regarding marriage and divorce can be applied here. That is, "If the shoe fits, wear it!" (My own paraphrase.)

Some of the people didn't need Jesus' teaching on divorce and remarriage because, obviously, if they were never married, divorce was not their problem. Likewise, if masturbation is not your problem, skip this whole dissertation. There are some who have very low sex drives. They require very little, if any, sexual gratification and can live without either masturbation or sexual involvements. There are others who range from moderate to extreme in their drives and desires, and it is to these I feel something should be said.

As already stated, sex is an important part of life. Walter and Ingrid Trobisch in *My Beautiful Feeling* explain one's sexuality as a language, a means of communication to another person. When you "talk" to yourself, it becomes lust directed toward oneself. "It divides a person in two, for he must play two incompatible roles simultaneously—that of the stimulus giver and stimulus receiver."

Your heart remains unsatisfied. And when gratification is the goal, gratification is rarely attainable—talking to oneself is rarely satisfying.

The apostle Paul, who had a lot to say to single people, wrote in 2 Corinthians 10:5: "[We are] Casting down imaginations, and every high thing that exalteth itself against the knowledge of God, and bringing into captivity every thought to the obedience of Christ" (KJV).

And again, he says in Philippians 4:8, ". . . Fix your thoughts on what is true and good and right. Think about things that are pure and lovely, and dwell on the fine, good things in others. Think about all you can praise God for and be glad about" (LB).

What am I trying to say by quoting these Scriptures? I'm saying practice self-control (part of the fruit of the Spirit) and be particular about what goes into your mind by way of literature, pictures, movies, TV, music, and the like.

I know of a man who spent his entire life fighting masturbation, until he finally thought he had it conquered. He got all excited and tried to write a book about his battle—giving the steps he decided it took to overcome the problem. His psychologist read the manuscript and calmly told him he hadn't solved any problem at all; he had just gotten older, and his body chemistry had changed. All that had happened was that in his older age his passions had lessened, and his self-control was easier to accomplish. One of the reasons he'd endured such a long fight was because he had masturbation on his mind constantly.

Constant concentration on *anything* is not healthy. The subject of concentration will soon become an obsession, and the individual tends to become enslaved by the very thing he has been trying to overcome. The man's problem was his focus of attention as much as it was masturbation. He had lost control of his passions partly because he concentrated so vigorously on *not* indulging.

Again, quoting Dr. and Mrs. Trobisch, they say:

> Prayer is always helpful, if it is an expression of our
> fellowship with God. But there is also a kind of prayer

which focuses on one point, on one single unfulfilled
human desire. This is only a caricature of prayer. If
you pray this way about masturbation, it does not
help. It is like driving at night. When you look straight
into the headlights of the oncoming car for fear of
crashing into it, it is very likely that you may do just
that.

Self-centered thoughts and prayers, whether on the subject
of sex or any other subjective emotion, are an invitation to
become imbalanced. What do you think about the most?
Chances are, your thoughts reveal your problem. We tend to
focus all our emotional energies on the thing that is causing us
the most difficulty, and so it's always looming in the forefront
of our conscious thoughts, causing conflicts.

Paul writes, "Casting down imaginations, and every high
thing that exalteth itself against the knowledge of God . . ."
(2 Corinthians 10:5 KJV). If self-gratification (not just masturbation) is a problem, you need to ask the Lord to help you
redirect your thinking and energies to someone or something
that is more needful of your time and efforts.

The Lord won't force your thinking, so when these thoughts
come, be conscious of them. If they are leading to some un-
controllable act, the action of self-discipline must be deliberate
to consciously change the thought patterns. Transferring a
self-centered activity or thought to another self-centered activity really isn't accomplishing any constructive purpose; your
thoughts are still on yourself. Books are written telling people
with sex problems to take cold showers or work out at a gym.
To my way of thinking, that is still self-centeredness. Certainly,
there are more important needs in the world than gratifying
oneself. That isn't to say that physical exercise doesn't help,
but it is only scratching the surface of the problem. We must
talk to the Lord about our problem with self-gratification and
use every means He provides to bring our thoughts into sub-
jection and to renew our minds (*see* Romans 12:1, 2).

Most importantly, one must develop a circle of friends who can minister as a group to one another and to individuals or groups that are needy. Expand your world to include those who are not as fortunate or gifted or healthy as you are. It's amazing how our personal problems become insignificant when seen in the light of some of the major problems other people have.

If we could only understand the prayer of St. Francis of Assisi, "Lord, make me an instrument of thy peace." We must reach out to be God's instrument of peace in a troubled society. But the world seems so large and foreboding, and we feel it's too big for us to handle. It is, so we must narrow that world down to our cities and our neighborhoods and our immediate circles of friends and family. We must join forces with other singles who have energy to give, and make *our* world a better place to live.

Then, as you've laid the whole thing at the feet of Jesus, and if you'd rather stay pure and chaste as a single Christian, let Him deal with your sexual needs. I believe that if a person can exercise control, then let him exercise control. If he cannot, then that could be why God never mentioned masturbation as sin.

Abstinence is probably best, but self-control must always be the rule. If there's no self-control, seek help from a sensitive Christian counselor. Admitting the problem is the first step in finding a solution. Going to the proper source for help is the second step. Don't suffer unnecessary confusion and guilt when help is available.

We can't be too judgmental on this. We can't make a law where there is none. We can't project guilt where an action is not mentioned as sin.

We *can* trust God to take care of our needs. If we are truly Spirit-filled people, then we have the supernatural power of God working in us. I honestly believe that God can supersede our natural cravings and preserve us and keep us happy and content in His own miraculous way.

Let's rejoice that, as we have the Holy Spirit living in us in His fullness, we are not limited to natural laws, but can be truly supernatural and rise above the conflicts and frustrations that plague so many single Christian adults today. Never underestimate the power and love of God. He wants you to remain healthy in spirit, soul, and body; and total and complete surrender to Him will assure peace and victory at the same time.

7

Homosexuality and God

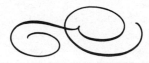

Newspapers and television talk shows, public demonstrations and debates: So many are screaming, "Gay rights! Liberation! God loves the homosexual!" Christians are reacting in fear, repulsion, confusion, and sometimes with attempts at understanding.

Major church denominations are ordaining admitted homosexuals to the active ministry. There is controversy everywhere on this issue. Borderlines that were once thought to be absolute are now becoming vague, and, to some, they are almost nonexistent!

While all of this is going on, very real people in Christian homes all across America, people with very real homosexual problems, are watching and searching and begging for answers to questions they've hidden for years.

While the Anita Bryant controversy in Miami was blaring across the nation, I was trying to answer a letter from a young woman who confided that she has strong lesbian tendencies that she has kept secret most of her life. She's married and a mother. She loves her family, but she sexually prefers women. The open publicity on the subject has given her the hope that she can "come out" and not be declared an unfit mother or a deviate of some sort.

Singles who have not been successful in developing relationships with the opposite sex entertain thoughts that they
may have latent homosexual tendencies, and, in search of love
and acceptance, they consider investigating such a liaison.
Singles who have fought homosexual tendencies all their lives
are breathing sighs of relief; now they can be free to relate to
the same sex. The public is learning that not all homosexuals
are child molesters or deviates or weirdos. Most hold down
normal jobs and mind their own business.

What is the real truth about homosexuality? Is it true that the
New Testament says nothing about homosexuality? That's
what the minister of the "gay" Los Angeles Metropolitan
Church says. He teaches that in the New Testament dispensa-
tion we are not bound by the Law, nor is our salvation dependent upon our keeping the Law. He teaches that homosexuality is not sin. And he's right about the Law and its relationship
to God's grace, love, and forgiveness.

But he is avoiding some very clear Scripture in Romans, in
the letters to the Corinthians, in Ephesians, and countless other
Scriptures where sexual sins are discussed and stringent
guidelines are laid out. Deviations from God's Law, no matter
how they are explained, are still called sin, and that's all there
is to that.

Recently a television crew in Los Angeles visited this gay
church and interviewed the members. Christians with listening
ears received insight and rebuke as they watched. Without
exception, the homosexuals all said they wanted to go to
church and worship God and be accepted as what they are:
gay. They said that "straight" churches either cast them out or
treat them with disdain, as second (or third or fourth) class
citizens. They knew they weren't welcome, and so they could
not worship in a "regular " church, especially if their "sexual
preference" was even suspected, and certainly not if it were
known for sure.

What a tragic indictment against the Church today, if their

charges are true. If the Church is unable to understand and minister, what other alternative do the gays have than to form their own church? If Christ's Church is unable to dispense love and forgiveness to sinners, where else can they find it?

I'm not saying that I condone the homosexuals banding together to form their own community of worship. But I *am* saying that unless the Church, with its hosts of counselors, receives people with deep-seated problems and tries to understand them spiritually and emotionally, those people will certainly go where they are not required to change before they are accepted. That's only realistic.

We who have experienced the renewing love of Jesus must allow the homosexual as much grace to be healed and changed in the inward man as God has allowed *us* through Christ Jesus. And we must give them the better alternative to homosexuality: the healing, cleansing love of Jesus, which is manifested through us.

As we (the Church) experience the grace of God that gives us love and understanding, we must also know and teach that homosexuality is definitely a sin: one that God would not tolerate in Sodom and Gomorrah. His Word says it's an abomination and unnatural (*see* Romans 1:26). However, because we know it is sin, that doesn't give us license to reject the sinner, pass judgment, and set the penalty. In fact, if we ask the Lord for a little understanding, we might see that we're not so different in our sins than the gays are in theirs.

We all know that it's easy to cast off guilt by saying that our pet vice is really "okay." It's a lot easier to justify our actions by declaring that we're an exception, living under grace and therefore allowed to sin. None of us want to be placed in the broad category of "common sinners." We find it easier to pretend we're not sinning than to accept the responsibility for our actions and at the same time accept the responsibility for making a change. That's our fallen-nature tendency—regardless of the sin.

Simply put, we cannot be judgmental of others' sins unless we use the same degree of judgment on ourselves.

In the few years that I've been counseling homosexuals, I've come to believe that most of them continue in their life-style because they think it's the only way for them. They have accepted their sexual preference as the only way they can be, and they try to make the best of it. Deceiving and insidious tools are used by the devil to cause those people to walk in exhausted defeat.

All of us have been hurt, and most of us have had very difficult emotional experiences in our backgrounds, but the evidence of those experiences in later life varies greatly. Homosexuality appears to be one of the consequences of many negative early-life experiences. Psychologists give many reasons to explain homosexual preference; they delve into the past and come up with a multiplicity of causes. Probably the most reasonable explanations involve experiences in childhood or an unfortunate homelife that had traumatic effects on the emotions of the growing youngster.

One young woman I know of was sexually attacked by a man when she was in grade school. Another had a child-beating father. Another had parents who were disappointed she wasn't a boy. A young man I've counseled was orphaned and brought up in a boys' home where he was introduced to homosexual acts by others in the home. Another had a father who was "too busy" to be interested in his children.

The tragedies go on endlessly. But whatever the causes, those deep hurts remain either as open sores or sensitive scar tissue. From all psychological viewpoints, most of the reasons for homosexuality appear to be emotionally legitimate, and the psychologist will do what he can to help the patient adjust.

Sometimes a homosexual will transfer his sense of guilt or blame and place the responsibility for the problem and the cure on his parents, or whomever he deems responsible.

But fingers of fault need not be pointed. Arms of love should be extended. Homosexuals are very real, very sensitive people. The love they have for one another is strong and, in their frame of reference, genuine. For some, it's the only kind of love they have ever known. Just as the heterosexual strives to have his wants and needs satisfied (not just sexually), so does the homosexual. It is just that the enemy took advantage of a very bad situation deep in the recesses of the emotional past and caused that scar tissue to fester, to be easily reopened, and to keep the person sensitive and frightened.

That's so much like Satan! He'll take a bad experience and make sure it stays with us forever. Not only the lingering, painful memory stays, but he'll make sure that mistrust, hate, fear, and self-centeredness accompany that memory.

The love experienced between homosexuals is real, but only within their realm of experience. Their "love" is not the quality of love God intended to be found in a marriage relationship; in the first chapter of Romans, verses 24 through 27, we're told that they have turned against God's natural plan for them.

When God created the human race, He created them "male and female," and they were told to cleave to one another and become one flesh. This is God's natural plan for male and female, and in their naturalness, they were to multiply and replenish the earth. "And God saw every thing that he had made, and, behold, it was very good . . ." (Genesis 1:31 KJV).

Though two people of the same sex may be experiencing what seems to be a fulfilling relationship, according to God's standard it is unnatural and *cannot* be fulfilling. Possibly, for a period of time, the individuals involved may feel they are "happy" or "blessed," and they vow to love one another till death parts them. But their happiness is based on an ungodly premise, and so it cannot be satisfying or permanent in God's creation.

Eventually, what seems to be love between homosexuals requires constant reinforcement by both parties. Whether the .

individuals involved realize it or not, the fact that gay love is unnatural causes much insecurity and jealousy, and the expressions of love often become bribes to keep the relationship going. There's always the fear that the desperately sought intimacy will end, and that insecurity creates terrible problems.

But then all that goes equally for illicit sex relationships between *heterosexuals*. When a couple experiences sex outside of marriage—even in the total belief that their relationship is true love—because it is outside the ordained plan of God, it is unnatural, and therefore temporary. As much as our modern ethics would like to change this principle, unless a man and woman have that "piece of paper" called a marriage license, there's not enough glue to stick the couple together. The premise is ungodly, and the parting comes quickly.

When sex is experienced outside the sanctified, natural laws of God, the motivation for it is self-gratification on the part of one or both of the partners. For the heterosexual, God intends marriage, by a special decree. The sex relationship can be called the "seal" that binds the vow. As we've seen, sex will bind individuals to each other, whether they want to be bound or not, but to be bound to someone without mental, spiritual, and legal consent can only create pressure that will one day pop the cork.

God isn't trying to make things hard on people; He's trying to make us conform to the image of His Son so we can have fellowship with the Creator, and that can only be done within the confines of His high standards. We are created to worship and praise Him in all that we do, and a life led contrary to His purposes is destined for defeat and ultimate destruction. His spiritual principles are *always* in operation. The impossibility of a homosexual relationship ever bringing praise and glory to God is surely the reason God calls it an abomination.

Most gays who have been exposed to the saving love of God want to experience His redemption and to walk in fellowship with Him. Many others shy away from Him because they don't see how they can change their ways. Those who choose God's way, I find, usually fall into similar categories.

First, there is what I call "the Romans Seven Syndrome." These gay people struggle because they know they ought to be against what they think they are. There is a battle going on, and they know they should win, but they find themselves doing the very thing they vowed they'd never do. Constant inner (and outer) struggles persist, until they cry out with Paul, "Wretched person that I am, who will deliver me?" (*See* Romans 7:24.)

Then there is the gay individual who knows he needs to get right with God but doesn't really want to give up his homosexual preference. He seems to want to be free from the inner turmoil and guilt but doesn't really want to give up the sin. He seems to be enjoying the sin, but he isn't enjoying the guilt or the very good possibility that God doesn't approve of what he is doing.

There are some who want to stop their sin, but they want God to do it for them. They pray before going to bed that God will take away the desire, and then the next day they repeat the same sin.

A young woman told me she had some friends who were willing to pray for her deliverance from lesbianism, but she was hesitant to have them pray because they couldn't *guarantee* a complete healing. I told her that the person praying can't guarantee a complete healing, but God can, *if* He has the full cooperation of the one being prayed for.

The easy way out and the pat answer is to "turn it over to Jesus." But I felt God wanted that gal to make up her own mind that she would have victory—with God's help. Any "guarantees" are dependent upon the decision *she* makes about which way *she* wants to go. If she is ready to go all the way with God, the complete healing is hers for the asking.

No one can expect God to do something that the individual must do: that is, make the choice. But if a person decides to go with God: that is, to let go of all the emotions and desires that have been so important and trust God for something they don't even understand, they will be "more than conquerors!"

Obviously, these principles are not "for gays only." All of us are guilty of secret sins and of hanging on to some pet habits that we think we can cover for by making it up to God in some other way. Or we just try to ignore the problem. But finally, each of us must be honest before God, accepting the responsibility to take the necessary action, in the power of God, to overcome the sin that so easily besets us.

If you are gay, God sees the longings and understands the desires of your heart. He knows what made you that way, and He knows what it takes to bring about your healing. If you are ready, God will perform miracles you need and give you the fortitude to see you through to the finish. It won't be easy—the devil will see to that. So before you go ahead with the Lord, you should count the cost.

In the fourteenth chapter of Luke, Jesus told His disciples that they had to count the cost before they decided to follow Him. He said a builder wouldn't begin construction on a building without first getting an estimate and then checking to see if he had enough money to pay the bills. Otherwise he might complete only the foundation and run out of funds.

There's a definite cost involved when you say "yes" to God. It may even turn out to be almost a struggle between life and death, and you will grow weary of fighting and praying. The problem is deeply ingrained, and the roots are often hidden and complicated. To promise quick deliverance or instant freedom is to build up false hopes that can lead to failure and discouragement.

And I think I must say with Greg Reid, former gay and now minister to homosexuals through Eagle Ministries, "Heterosexuality is not the answer to homosexuality. Struggles and attempts to change sexual preference create more frustration and brokenness. Wholeness is the goal."

Aren't you glad He came for that reason?

I can't forget the story Jesus tells in Luke 18 about the insistent widow who wouldn't quit asking the Master to meet her need. The New American Standard Bible puts the first verse of that chapter this way: ". . . [Men] ought to pray and not to lose heart." That concept really jumped out at me. How often do we lose heart in our fight and give up the battle? Maybe our giving up comes just moments before we would have experienced victory!

The devil doesn't give up easily, and he doesn't leave under the proper rules of protocol. He has to be *commanded* to go in the power and the Name of Jesus, and we have to keep after him until he knows who is boss! We are not to lose heart in the battle, but to fight him with every tool God has given us. The devil knows he's lost the battle, even before he begins, and his bluff only works when we believe we can't win!

Because Christians are in the flesh, they will always have a problem with sin. Our guilt tells us, "I alone am overwhelmed by secret sins!" Our feeling of exclusivity with sin makes us draw into ourselves and struggle alone—and often lose the battle.

God *has* made us uniquely individual, but all human flesh is very much the same. The Scripture says, "There hath no temptation taken you but such as is *common* to man . . ." (1 Corinthians 10:13 KJV, *italics added*). That means sin is common, but answers are common, too!

Submit to Jesus Christ and His perfect will for your life! It sounds trite, and we've all heard it before, but no truer statement can ever be made! He is the Healer, the Deliverer, and He came to set the captive free and to give an abundant life!

8
The Liberation Myth

When I first began considering how to approach the subject of women's liberation, I imagined myself coming against the Gloria Steinems, Betty Friedans, and others who are making shrieking noises for the liberation of women.

There are many reasons why I'm unable to argue with these women. Probably, if I came face-to-face with one of them in debate, she would totally reject my statements and scorn me right out of the room. She and I are so different because, as a Christian, I have an authoritative premise upon which I build my beliefs. The women's-liberation premise is built upon the frustrations that come from a sense of unfulfillment and insecurity in a society that is built upon anti-God values, standards, and concepts.

Since each woman proclaiming equality with men is uniquely individual herself (because God has created each of us different), not even the most committed advocates of women's lib can fully agree with one another on very many issues. Each one has her own premise, based on her own subjective observations and experiences. Consequently, within the liberation ranks there are disagreements and undefined goals.

Gradually, as I contemplated the issues, my whole attitude

changed. It's not the unsaved women's-lib advocates I want to
address; it is the Christian person who has believed the propaganda of *any* liberation movement whose whole basis of discontent is straight from the enemy of our soul.

It is our enemy who seeks to create dissatisfaction and
restlessness by taking our thoughts off the Great Liberator,
Jesus Christ, and putting them on inward, self-oriented demands. Satan's ways are more diversified than we'll ever be
able to know, and we must be alert to his tactics; but more
than that, we must be thoroughly acquainted with what God's
Word has to say about true liberation.

I think I'm safe in assuming that some of us women believe
that the church has discriminated against us, and certainly we
are safe in stating that society and the business world have
some discriminatory habits toward women.

Where civil rights are concerned, the outspoken proponents
have succeeded in getting many much-needed "equal rights"
passed on both the federal and state levels. Men and women
of all ages and races are securely protected, by law, against
discrimination.

I have to agree that men and women are equal in worth, if
it's a value judgment one is making. But the difficulty arises
when they attempt to propagate "sameness." I'm glad we're
not the same. Not only are physical differences acutely obvious, so are desires, drives, and aptitudes. (That could be a
good reason for needing each other.)

NBC Television did a special documentary on the changing
roles of men and women in society over the past century; it
told the story of creation as it was rewritten by a "liberated"
woman. She attempted to show a woman other than Eve as
created for Adam. This commentator would have us believe
that the first woman God gave Adam was "equal" with Adam,
and a conflict resulted over who would be the dominant personality. Lilith, Adam's first wife in this yarn, was independent,
self-sufficient, and not submissive to Adam's desires. Sup-

posedly, Adam, already a chauvinistic male, complained to God, asking for a woman who would not compete for dominance. The answer to Adam's prayer? Eve. A quiet, submissive, docile woman whom Adam could control.

The story did not end happily, according to this version. Lilith, whom Adam forced out of the Garden so Eve could enter, eventually returned and convinced Eve that she was being discriminated against, and her rights were being violated. They walked off together into the sunset to dominate and grow and control the earth.

Unfortunately, in some Christian seminaries and churches, many nonscriptural thoughts are being heard and written on the liberation issue. Women want to assume roles of leadership that have either traditionally been held by men or are specifically reserved for men in the Scriptures. Denominations are splitting over this issue, and harsh and unloving words are being spoken.

It seems that some people are trying to create their own God (in their own images) who will not make them uncomfortable in the roles they have chosen to play (and don't we all do that!). What is so sad is that these people don't know the God who created them in *His* image (not male nor female, but in spirit and potential). And they don't appreciate His Son, who has set them free from the curse that came upon them when Eve believed Satan's lies about being liberated from ignorance. The enemy is still telling the same lies. He told Eve she could be like God and know good and evil if she'd just eat that forbidden fruit. He's still trying to convince Christians that God didn't really mean what He said, and that sin really isn't sin. Eve learned about evil in a big hurry, as soon as she disobeyed. I'm sure if she could talk to us today, she'd let us know that we'd be a lot better off if she hadn't acquired that knowledge of good and evil. And she'd apologize and ask forgiveness from all her children for exposing us to the wiles of that serpent!

Even after Adam and Eve so miserably failed and God kept His word and put them out of the Garden, His mercy still ruled with His justice. He had to keep His word, but He made a provision for them even then: the first blood sacrifice to cover the nakedness of "man." Their nature, which was originally made in the very image of God, now became a penitent one. Eve would experience sorrow and pain in bearing children, and her desires would be "for her husband," and he would rule over her. "Them's the facts, folks": the results of disobedience.

But, women, don't feel sorry for yourselves yet; we didn't actually get the worst of it. Men had to begin to toil and sweat and couldn't eat unless they worked for each mouthful! Hard labor became a way of life. That's not all that happened, of course, but it represents a start at understanding why we're even in the predicament we're in.

But again, God's mercy prevails. At the same time His creatures let Him down, He promised that one would come who would trample the enemy, and Satan became the cursed one (*see* Genesis 3:15).

Women have been told since then that they are living under curses: the monthly menstruations are a curse; obeying one's husband is a curse; sex is a curse; housework is a curse; and on and on it goes. Women have believed those myths, and also believed that they were in every way the weaker sex; so they have, generally speaking, acquiesced, until recently. Men have believed the dogma, too, and now that women are making more demands and exerting their independence and strengths, men don't know how to react to these new attitudes. Women's fashions are changing to become more and more masculine; women are demanding that men assume some of the responsibility in household chores and child care; women want positions of employment that have been traditionally open to men only, with equal pay, too. Women are transferring their motherhood responsibilities to child-care centers or baby-sitters; they are moving out into the world to achieve equality and fulfillment.

I really don't want to talk about the rightness or wrongness of those attitudes. What I want to discover is if it's really true that women are living under some sort of curse, and particularly Christian women.

I checked my authoritative premise, the Manufacturer's Handbook, to learn if God really does intend women to be second-class citizens—that is, subject to and under the rule of man—and was very pleasantly surprised at what I found. Look up *woman* in your Bible concordance and see what women have had to do in the history of "humankind."

For those women who want equal jobs today—you aren't saying anything new. In the Old Testament, women had jobs that broke what we call the "sex stereotype" barrier; they kept vineyards, herded flocks, tended fields, were doorkeepers, had specific tasks in the temple. They held political positions, aided in war, were queens, prophetesses, and were most influential in the lives of their men and in the decisions they made.

I even found a case of women's lib in Numbers 27, where a father died, leaving no male heir. According to law, that meant the estate would go to the man's surviving brothers, but his daughters protested, saying they rightfully deserved the inheritance. The daughters protested to Moses, and the patriarch consulted God about the matter. The Almighty made an exception to the law and gave the inheritance to the daughters!

The most profound biblical description of a well-rounded, liberated, successful woman is given by Solomon in the final chapter of Proverbs. Solomon was a connoisseur of women, and he painted a picture of a woman that should be the standard for us all.

Some of God's laws were hard on women (men, too), and we don't understand the whys and wherefores of a lot of them. The justice of God always prevailed, and those who were found guilty of breaking the laws were punished in ways God had established and announced in advance.

But God is not a merciless taskmaster, laying down laws just to watch us squirm in defeat and frustration. Believing women, even under the Law, were treated by God as most worthy beings. They received protection and status that pagan women could never attain.

It should mean a lot to Christian women that God chose a woman to bring forth the Messiah, even though He could have been spontaneously created. There were important women in the lineage of Jesus, and some women who were of questionable repute. (Isn't it so like our God that He is not a respecter of persons and keeps His promises? When He forgives sins, He doesn't hold them against us any longer.) Jesus, the Son of God, born of a woman, came to liberate all of us, male and female, from the curse of sin and death. "Christ redeemed us from the curse of the Law, having become a curse for us . . ." (Galatians 3:13 NAS). "For if the ministry of condemnation has glory, much more does the ministry of righteousness abound in glory" (2 Corinthians 3:9 NAS).

Because of Jesus, we have a better way than the women of the Old Testament. Under the Law, they were still able to perform marvelous feats, and were in no way limited because they were women (but only because of the curse of sin that the Law demanded). The New Testament provides even more possibilities for women, because Jesus is the Great Liberator who provided the truest liberation. ". . . where the Spirit of the Lord is, there is liberty" (2 Corinthians 3:17 NAS). "If therefore the Son shall make you free, you shall be free indeed" (John 8:36 NAS). We are free from bondage and the cares of this world, free to fulfill all the potential God gave us.

Jesus fulfilled the Law by proclaiming that the Kingdom of heaven was at hand. "If you have died with Christ to the elementary principles of the world, why, as if you were living in the world, do you submit yourself to decrees . . . ?" (Colossians 2:20 NAS.)

How confused we get when we form our values and life-styles according to the opinions of people in the world: people whose standards rest only on their own, subjective, self-willed, highly limited knowledge and experience. We are told that we aren't to be conformed to this world, but to be transformed by renewing our minds (*see* Romans 12:2). And Jesus prayed that the Father would not take us out of the world, but that we would be kept safe from the evil one.

We are citizens of a Kingdom that is *not* of this world (*see* John 18:36). We are royalty: children of God, joint heirs of the Firstborn Son, who is the Prince of Peace. The Prince of Peace is either ruling in our hearts, or we are still struggling with the hopeless effort to reconcile the world we live in with His Kingdom. The two are simply not compatible because the Kingdom of God is righteousness and peace and joy in the Holy Spirit (*see* Romans 14:17). The Kingdom of God is that life or situation in which Jesus reigns as Lord and King. But the kingdom of the world is ruled by the prince of the power of the air: a liar and the father of lies, a murderer, seeking whom he may destroy.

And so, in whose kingdom do you really live?

In this world, every minority group imaginable is demanding its specialized rights, and, in this world, people *do* have rights. But since we believers are *not* of this world, what are *our* rights? Let's look at the rights of the heavenly Kingdom.

There's a lot of information in the Bible about the Kingdom of God. Jesus said the Kingdom of God is in our hearts, "righteousness and peace and joy." He gave illustrations explaining the Kingdom, and we don't properly understand most of them. John the Baptist and the disciples preached the "Gospel of the Kingdom."

Pursuing the ideal liberation, I went through my concordance and other reference materials and was going to do a big study on the Kingdom of God, pointing out all the attributes of the Kingdom, what one has to do to maintain citizenship, and that it is surely ruled with righteousness (*see* Hebrews 1:8). But there's a lot of doctrine in that study, and greater commentators than I have attempted to understand and teach the concepts of the Kingdom of God, I found. I finally decided to leave that kind of research to those who have the required gifts.

But as I had been studying the Kingdom of God and trying to establish a definition that was at least satisfactory to me, my thoughts kept going to the One who is the ruler of the Kingdom, and the verse that says, "The disciple is not above his master, nor the servant above his lord. It is enough for the disciple that he be as his master, and the servant as his lord . . ." (Matthew 10:24, 25 KJV).

And this takes us right to Jesus and the big questions, "What were His rights in the Kingdom while He was in the world?" "Was *He* liberated?"

We're so determined to get our rights. We feel we have a right to this or that. We even think we have a right to lose our tempers at someone who "deserves a piece of our minds." We covet our "rightful places" in the church or on the job or in the home. We demand our rights as if all that mattered in this life was a guarantee of our own inalienable right to the pursuit of our own happiness.

Jesus, the One who knew no sin became sin that we might be made the righteousness of God in Him (*see* 2 Corinthians 5:21). It was Jesus, "Who, being in the form of God, thought it not robbery to be equal with God: But made himself of no reputation, and took upon him the form of a servant . . ." (Philippians 2:6, 7 KJV). Jesus, who had the "right" to be in heaven, ruling with God, who had a "right" to everything that we think is important, *willingly forfeited His rights so we can be counted worthy to be citizens of His Kingdom.*

Our minds can't comprehend, can't adequately grasp, the shabby comparison between our petty demands for our rights and His magnificent sacrifice. He died to His rights—not on the cross, but when He made the decision to leave His rights behind and become flesh. There was a world to save, and He established His priorities. He chose to forfeit both His heavenly and His earthly rights to save the world He loved.

We go around parading, protesting, debating, and lauding worldly reasoning, when Jesus said, ". . . Except a corn of wheat fall into the ground and die, it abideth alone . . ." (John 12:24 KJV). When was Jesus finally able to be glorified and claim His rights? After He completed the work the Father called Him to do. Read about it in John 12 and 17:4, 5. Jesus died, alone, like that small corn of wheat: ". . . but if it die, it bringeth forth much fruit." "He that loveth his life shall lose it; and he that hateth his life in this world shall keep it unto life eternal" (John 12:24, 25 KJV).

There's a strange paradox in the Christian walk. To die means abundant life. To be in bondage means complete freedom. To be least means to be the greatest. To give means to receive. To be last is to be the first. To be meek is to inherit the earth. To be His servant is to be set free, to be really liberated.

All the time we're looking for joy and peace, it's available in the Kingdom of God—*that life where Jesus is King.*

The degree to which we die is the degree to which we are liberated. When you're dead, nothing matters anymore. When you can be so free from the cares of the world that nothing out there matters, then you're really free. Not free from responsibilities, but free of every "right" that would keep you from the righteousness, joy, peace, and true liberation in the Holy Spirit.

9
Reality

Almost from the beginning of time, every young girl has been expected to have some worthwhile material possessions, once called a *dowry,* to offer a husband at the time of their marriage. In fact, the worth of the dowry was part of the marriage contract, and the more valuable that dowry, the better her father's bargaining power was in getting the right match for her.

Somewhere in the course of time, the custom of the dowry changed, and the parents stopped choosing the marriage partners for their children. But the custom of the girl having pretty and practical household items put away for her marriage lingered on. Her possessions were no longer called a dowry, and they weren't used for bargaining power in the marriage contract. The dowry became a *hope chest* that was filled with lovely, homemade marriage necessities.

The dowry and hope chest have waned with the passing of time, but the hope of marriage is here to stay. Young people are still filled with dreams for a happily-ever-after marriage, and this is not really the influence of the parents. From generation to generation, a girl and boy have been expected by society in general to marry, have a family, and be happy. And that's as it should be, because God ordained marriage, making the man-woman relationship a fundamental part of life.

Consequently, most singles live in, and for, the future—for that great, new day when wedding bells will ring and those cherished hopes will be fulfilled.

Many Christian young people go to Bible schools or join college-career groups at church with the intention of finding a Christian mate. And surely, there's no better place to find a Christian mate than at a Christian college or church. College days should be days of dating and planning, learning and growing and dreaming, for both men and women. They're a time to sort out feelings and learn what one really needs in a lifetime mate.

However, we "post-graduates" who are still hanging on to that "someday in the future" could be facing real tragedy.

What happens to the here and now when we're *not* married? *Now,* after all, is reality.

When I was in my early twenties, I bought china and cookwear, and my friends immediately jumped to the conclusion that my current steady date and I were planning marriage. My flip reply was, "Old maids have to eat, too, you know." Of course, I used the term "old maid" lightly, because I was twenty-two and certainly not an "old maid." Nor was I planning to become one.

Well, I kept all my precious goods in their original packing boxes for several years, saving them for my future marriage. I embroidered tablecloths and napkins and even bought a secondhand cedar chest to store them in.

Tonight, many years later, I served a dinner which was cooked in my cookwear, served on my china, and eaten with Betty Crocker Coupon silverware, which was set on my hand-embroidered linen tablecloth. It was a delightful evening, and I'm thankful I didn't wait for marriage before I rescued those pretty things from my hope chest. If I had waited, I'm sure they would have become badly tarnished, discolored, and mildewed. My hope chest surely would have turned into a "despair chest."

Tragically, there are many men and women who are storing up hopes in the region of the *physical* chest (heart), and too often, the hopes have turned to despair.

We store up so much inside us for the time when we will be married. We go to seminars on marriage and the family. The pastor preaches a series on family life, and we're in the front row, taking notes. The abundance of study materials on the subject of the family, submission, and the divine order of the marriage relationship is staggering. We learn all of these great truths so we will be the best marriage partner in the known world. Married people are in the majority, and pastors preach to that segment of the congregation most of the time. But there are nearly 50 million singles in our country today, and I'm glad God has made a place in the body of Christ for all of us.

We don't really have to store up a bundle of knowledge and then wait a long time before we can put it to use. That's not living with reality.

Oral Roberts for years has been talking about "Jesus in the now," and I never fully understood what he meant. But one day I talked with a young divorcée who was determined to believe that everything that happened in her life was in preparation for the new husband God would give her. And every guy she met was a candidate, as far as she was concerned. As I observed and listened, I saw something very common among unmarried adults— living in an ongoing state of being unsettled and feeling that all of life at the present is only marking time until . . . .

But, oh, how God wants to minister to us *now,* in the single state, so we can be content, so we can grow and learn of Him and be like Him . . . *now!*

Singles usually live in furnished apartments, or those who do choose to furnish do so with "Goodwill rejects." Why? Because, "Someday, when I'm married, *we'll* choose *our* furniture *together.*" So they continue to live in a place that can hardly be called a home, and they don't really even like to go there, except perhaps to sleep.

Singles also have the habit of changing jobs frequently, changing churches, changing roommates, changing apartments—driven by some inner force that refuses to accept their single status. A restlessness pervades their minds because of the nagging anticipation that "someday" everything will be different. "Someday" the right one will come. So round and round they go, ever hoping to stop "someday."

It's no wonder insurance agencies and loan and credit companies are reluctant to do business with singles.

How do I know about this? I've been there. But it would take too long to list all of my jobs and former addresses and disappointments. Suffice it to say that during a very long period of time I waited for God's will for my life to unfold. I couldn't accept my single status as being God's will, because I was waiting for a husband to come along so I could be a *helpmeet* and serve the Lord.

So I continued to wait, sort of treading water, wondering what a single woman could possibly do in Christian work, other than the stereotyped Sunday-school teacher, volunteer worker, Christian education director, and so forth. My thoughts of ministry and Christian service were geared to activities, and I felt that *doing* things was extremely limited for a woman. In other words, my despair chest was full and running over.

Recently, however, there's been a change. I've been accused of "resigning" myself to *never* getting married, because I have said that I now accept my single status as being God's will for my life. Besides, single is not necessarily a permanent condition.

Let me say, though, that acceptance of the *now* is not resignation to something that is unavoidable. It is rather a total confidence that God knows what He is doing, and I know that He is in control of my life. It took me a long time to get to this trusting relationship with Him, but now my life is His to do with as He pleases. Should I then be so presumptuous to imply that He has made a mistake in having me remain single?

Selfish minds that we have, He is so much more concerned that we allow ourselves to know *Him.* He wants us to seek Him and His Kingdom *now!* And to let Him add on the other things we have need of (He promised to supply *all* our needs!) in His way and in His time (*see* Matthew 6:33).

Seek the Kingdom? How? What is it?

Jesus said the Kingdom is within us—now! It is fulfilled in us through the indwelling of the Holy Spirit. Paul said the Kingdom of God is righteousness and peace and joy in the Holy Ghost (*see* Romans 14:17). God's Kingdom is that realm (life) in which Jesus is King! *Now.* In us! As long as we keep on searching for the "perfect will of God" in every conceivable place, activity, or person, we'll miss the righteousness, peace, and joy every time. If we found it, we probably wouldn't recognize it, because we wouldn't know what we were looking for in the first place.

One day, in my search to relieve the despair, I went to hear a minister speak on the subject "God's will for your life." How many times I'd heard a sermon by that title and read books on the subject, just wanting to learn how to know God's will. So I listened; I probably expected him to come forth with a word of prophecy, speaking dramatically in an echo chamber, *"Ye shall be chosen from many to . . . ."* But, instead, he read from Romans 8:29, ". . . he also did predestinate [us] to be conformed to the image of his Son . . ." (KJV).

What? That's too simple! I want specifics, like what job should I take? Where is my husband? What will I be doing in ten years?

But the pastor expounded, and I studied, and eventually I learned what God had been trying to teach me all along—that His will for my life is simply "to be conformed to the image of his Son"! *Now!*

It sounds simple, but it's not a simple process to get there.

Our minds are geared to glamorous activities: huge throngs of people being saved and healed. We want the exciting, dynamic gifts of the Spirit manifested in our lives, to convince us that we're in His will and can be used by Him. But here I see that right now I'm supposed to be like Jesus. And all the time I thought that His will meant *doing* something. But it means *being!* And being is in the now! Doing can be put off indefinitely!

Living in the now requires being content in whatever state we're in. It requires that we fulfill our calling to be like Jesus *now!* We don't "resign" ourselves to living in the here and now as drudgery or punishment. There's no sad resignation to anything. There is *acceptance* of God's perfect love for us and, therefore, acceptance that where we are is where He wants us to be. If we can't accept and trust Him now, as single people, how can we accept, or even recognize, whatever He has for us in the future?

We can place no requirements on Jesus. He fulfilled His ultimate requirement on Calvary. *Now* we accept Him by believing, accepting, trusting, and obeying. If there is to be a change in the state we're in, praise God! But let Him do it! Not because we've searched for relief from our despair, but because we've sought Him and found Him.

We must be careful that we don't hold ourselves back spiritually for a ministry we think is yet to come. Let's not let our spiritual linens (gifts) become mildewed and consequently require difficult cleaning and renewing before they are fit to be used. Silver, when unused, tarnishes and becomes unpleasant to look at and difficult to clean. Let's not miss the joy of now by taking thought for tomorrow.

Our spiritual hope chest should not be full of things for the future, but overflowing with the gifts and fruit of the Spirit that come only with complete conformity to the image of Christ! Now! As a secretary, a clerk, a nurse, a teacher: whatever the "state," we are called to "be"—*now!*

10

The Bridegroom Comes

God calls the Church the "Bride of Christ."

When we, His body, said "yes" to His proposal of eternal life, we really said, "I do"! We made a vow that said, "I commit myself to You, in sickness and in health, to love and to cherish, honor and obey . . . ." And with this kind of commitment, we assumed a responsibility—a responsibility to live the life of His "Bride."

That was a startling revelation to me—not new, by any means, but it was quickened to me one evening when I was speaking to a group of Sunday-school teachers. I heard myself saying, "If some of you are as unfaithful to your mates as you are to the Lord, they have cause for divorce. When you gave your vows to one another, you really gave up all your rights as a private, selfish, personal individual and took on the responsibility and privilege of a partnership. Now you are married! You may not feel married all the time, but you are! Wives, the meals must be prepared, the clothes laundered, the house cleaned, whether you feel like it or not. Husbands, the finances must be met, the car kept in repair, the little odd jobs around the house done; it's part of the package deal in marriage.

"You're married because of mutual love and the vow you

117

gave. Nothing will change that commitment or the responsibility that comes with it. In a marriage relationship, responsibility often supersedes the rights of the individual, because your family requires time and energy and resources that would often preferably be spent on private thoughts, time, or projects. But the rights were surrendered with the commitment and consequent responsibility."

I guess I was really preaching that sermon to myself, because the moment I spoke those words, I realized how immeasurably patient God had been with me all these years. When I've sung "I Surrender All," all the time I meant, "I surrender *part* of my time." I was really saying, "I surrender to You the part of me that I know about. I surrender the future that I can foresee." I even went so far as to assume the attitude, "I'll surrender if You'll just show me what I'm surrendering to."

What kind of marriage relationship could a couple have with all the reservations inflicted upon it that I had put upon my relationship with Jesus? It seems to me there would be a lot of stress and insecurities and not much hope for real success.

Well, that's the way it was with me and Jesus in our relationship.

All my adult life I've heard it said that we singles should say that Jesus is our husband, our happiness, and I've agreed, in principle, to that. I'm sure, in my limited knowledge and experience, I thought He was. But since it is difficult to relate that spiritual concept to practical, personal living, and our earthbound physical and emotional functions, we doubt that God can take care of that part of us. We question how one can be married to Christ in any but a vague, figurative way. We probably take this "marriage to Christ" concept as an illustration to make a point, rather than a reality.

Ephesians, chapter 5, is a reference used to teach husbands and wives their responsibilities in the home and church. But I believe there is more for singles in that passage than we have allowed ourselves to see. Paul says in verse 32 that human marriage illustrates the *mystery* of the Church's relationship to Jesus. Something heretofore not understood (*mystery*) has been made clear to us: God's relationship through Jesus to us.

The human marriage relationship of love, commitment, caring, and responsibility that is appropriately demonstrated between husband and wife is an earthly example of the love relationship between Jesus and His Bride. And this example can also be reversed. If we have the slightest understanding of the love of Jesus toward us, and His purifying, beautifying, glorifying care, we can understand a little bit of how God really intends a human marriage to operate.

This Scripture also tells us that what we human beings have been looking for in a human relationship can be fully met in our relationship with Jesus!

As singles, we often forfeit that total union with Christ because we think that in order to be complete and fulfilled we *must* have a union with another person. The result is that our desires and prayer lives are consumed with thoughts of personal satisfaction and relief. In the natural state that is understandable and acceptable because that's the way we're made. Voices come screaming out to us, "It isn't natural to be alone!" "God intended man and woman to be together in marriage." "Why can't we have both—the union with Christ *and* with a human partner?"

God says you *can* have both, and most people do, though they often do not experience all of the oneness with God that is available. But since singles live in an unnatural state, we have to learn how to live in it as successful, rejoicing, and fulfilled Christians. It *is* possible, because since I am a child of God's, I'm no longer subject to the mere *natural!* I am *supernatural*, and therefore can live above the lonely tendencies of my own human nature.

Some people don't want Jesus to be their fulfillment because they've already made up their minds that a person, place, or thing will bring them ultimate satisfaction. With this point of view, there can never be satisfaction because the person, place, or thing upon which they have placed these responsibilities can never live up to their requirements. Therefore, there will always be disappointment in each relationship until Jesus becomes the ultimate satisfaction.

So, if Jesus is truly our satisfaction, let's look at what He will do for us as our "partner," if we will drop the barriers and receive Him in all His fullness.

The passage in Ephesians 5:25, 26 says, "Christ gave himself," not just to get us to heaven, but also to sanctify and cleanse us with "the washing of water by the word," and to beautify us and present us before Him in glory, without spot or wrinkle. We are nourished and cherished by Him because we are members of His body and flesh (verse 30). Just as no man ever yet hated his own flesh, Jesus loves His body and takes good care of it. And that means you and me—His body! He's making us into "beautiful people."

For this cause Jesus left His Father, so that we can be "one with Him." Notice the parallel:

> For this cause shall a man leave his father and mother, and cleave to his wife; And they twain shall be one flesh: so then they are no more twain, but one flesh. What therefore God hath joined together, let not man put asunder.
>
> Mark 10:7–9 KJV

And Jesus prayed, "That they all may be one; as thou, Father, art in me, and I in thee, that they also may be one in us . . ." (John 17:21 KJV).

Our union with Christ makes us one with Him, just as He and the Father are one. He uses the human marriage as His means of opening our understanding, just a little bit, to the glorious relationship He wants to have with us.

We tend to set human marriage up as the ultimate achievement for satisfaction and happiness, but we're seeing that our relationship with Christ is promising that. We're also seeing all around us that marriage can be destructive rather than constructive, and temporary rather than permanent. Today's statistics on marriage aren't very encouraging and should tell us not to rush into it carelessly, because, obviously, marriage is not the cure-all we might hope it is.

Believe me, I know how difficult it is to honestly submit to a life of being single. Don't think for a minute that I haven't struggled with this, and I still have setbacks, but by now anxiety is not a common emotional state for me. As mortals we seem to think we need acceptance and flattery and companionship, and I'm one of those mortals. Sometimes we go through long dry spells, and I must admit that I've wondered if there was something wrong with me, or if I had even as much "sex appeal" as a wet mop. Thank God, the dry spells are becoming fewer and fewer as I've begun to learn to trust my "Bridegroom" to be my fulfillment.

I know that it isn't natural to be alone. I'm aware that the feelings that come over a person alone at night, in the thundering silence, often seem unbearable. Eating dinner alone, watching TV alone, the stillness after the lights go out—all this can really defeat a person. But those are pretty shaky reasons for marriage. So the prayers still go up for a partner to talk to and love. A longing for a warm human being to touch and talk to and share with is a legitimate longing. But until that longing can be satisfied naturally, in God's perfect timing, there must be a way to live in the freedom and joy of the Lord without the heavy clouds of incompleteness hanging overhead.

And believe me when I say that there is a way!

For years I've heard dear old ladies give their testimonies about how they love God more and more, and how He gets "sweeter as the years go by," and a lot more of what I thought of as sentimental prattle about God. I thought their advanced age made them a little softheaded and forgetful of their youth, and those excitements and sorrows of the younger years. And I certainly didn't think they could be experiencing any of "life" as an elderly person, so, of course, they *would* think life with Christ was sweeter and better!

But now I see a bit more clearly what they're talking about, and I'm hardly in the "old age" category as yet.

I can see the personality and characteristics of God now, rather than just how He demonstrates His love to me. He sees the total picture; He knows what I'll be when I am old. He knows what experiences I need to prepare me for advancing age and to bring me into my total and fulfilled ministry. He knows the end, but I only know now. What I think I need now may be completely wrong for whatever situation I'll face later.

I am beginning to appreciate God the Father, and I think it is because I'm getting to know Him better. It must be kind of like a husband-wife relationship; the longer they live with each other, the more they know one another, how each operates and how each loves.

With God, the longer you live with Him and know Him, the more you love Him. Not because of how good He is to you, but because of how good He is, period!

The anthem "My Eternal King" puts it beautifully: "My God I love Thee, not because I hope for heaven thereby."

So now I know why the little old ladies are saying He grows sweeter every day. He does, because we know Him better and we see His love and wisdom and nature, and we know that He is our Lord and God and Eternal King, developing His ultimate best in our lives.

Because of that, I know Romans 8:28 is true. I know that even our sad and confusing times are accomplishing His purpose in us. I know I can trust Him in all things.

Jesus the Bridegroom, our covering and protector! There's a lot being said about that concept of the ministry of the Holy Spirit, particularly in reference to single women. There are

some who say that the woman's place in the church is second-
ary, and every woman must be submitted to a man. I don't
think that is entirely scriptural, because Paul says, "*wives* submit yourselves unto your own *husbands* . . . ." Unmarried
men and women don't fit either of those categories.

Of course, each and every one of us needs someone upon
whom we can depend for counsel, comfort, protection, and
the everyday human requirements. A human being is created
with the need to love and be loved. One of the reasons for that
need is that God can fill it. It has been called a "God-shaped
void"; only God can fit into it and fill it completely. But there is
the need for human ministry, too. The Scripture makes it clear
that we are to minister to one another, so if anyone feels a
need for that, it's normal! We know that the husband is the
natural fulfillment for the wife, and Christ is the covering for the
husband and the two—husband and wife.

This is where Ephesians 5 teaches so much. What the husband is to do for the wife, Christ is doing for the single person.
The twenty-fourth verse says the Church is subject to Christ;
that means you and I, who are the Church, are fulfilled and
completed by Christ, the Bridegroom. Christ loved the Church
(you and me) and gave Himself for us (the husband is supposed to do this for the wife). Christ is sanctifying and cleansing and washing us by the Word. He is presenting us as glorious, without spot or wrinkle, so that we can be holy and without blemish. He is nourishing and cherishing us personally,
because we are members of His body.

That should be exciting! Being personally ministered to by
Jesus Christ is no small thing! Paul said a great deal in 1
Corinthians, the seventh chapter, when he said that we single
people can be more sensitive to God's voice when we have
Jesus Himself doing the work in us. I really believe that we
single people have an advantage because married women, for
example, must let their imperfect husbands minister these

things to them, while we have Jesus Christ Himself meeting our needs and purifying us for His Kingdom!

As members of the body of Christ, we (male and female) are to submit to our pastor and the elders in our particular congregations. They are our spiritual leaders, and we are to go to them for counsel and leadership. In the Christian spirit and way of life, they are to minister to widows (which can include single women, too) and help with their needs.

Does all this fit the man, too? Paul said that the head of every man is Christ. The male human being is not an overpowering lord, king of the jungle, as centuries of traditions have taught us to believe.

When you get right down to it, a man's inner being has the same requirements as a woman's. He needs to be loved, cherished, protected, and nourished as much as the "weaker sex." Human society has had the mistaken idea that submission is a weakness. Men were taught to be "he-men" and not to cry or feel or care. And so the tender, gentle, meek traits of Jesus took on a negative tone, relegating our Lord, for some, to a world of women and weakness. But in the final analysis, it took greater strength than any earthly man has ever known for Jesus to submit Himself to the authorities and choose to suffer the humiliation of His ignominious death. He is a real man! And never forget, Jesus was a *single* man who was subject to His Father and was in absolute and complete surrender to Him for our sakes.

Yes, a man can have the same covering and protection and love and submission to Jesus as a woman does. The *same* commitment and submission is required of men as is required of women. Perhaps in this realm, we should remember that in Jesus there is no Greek or Jew, no bond or free, no male or female (*see* Galatians 3:28). Therefore, our needs are the same and the answer to those needs is the same.

It all boils down to this: the single person *is* living unnaturally. God intended men and women to marry and become

one and to function as a coordinated unit. God may or may
not bring mates into our lives. It would be good if He did in
many respects, but there are definite handicaps in being married, too. However, since it is unnatural to be single, and that's
the state we're now in, we have to rise above nature and live
supernaturally. This is possible only through the indwelling
power of the Holy Spirit. I believe it takes more discipline for
singles to walk in the Spirit, since we can't blame an imperfect
partner for our faults. But we can know that God won't call us
to do or be anything we can't successfully accomplish.

God has called some, I'm sure, to a life of being single; and it
isn't easy. But He has given us all the grace to fulfill our calling,
and not only are we reaping our rewards now but will continue
to be rewarded in the life to come, if we accept His gift (*see*
Luke 18:29, 30).

Jesus, the Bridegroom, loves the Church, His Bride, and
gave Himself for her. The Church is made up of all those
people we characteristically separate into different segments of
society. I don't believe He sees us as married or unmarried,
divorced or widowed, male or female; He sees us as needy,
vulnerable, lonely, hurting people who need the comforting,
fulfilling ministry of the Holy Spirit. He has promised to give
His Spirit to all who ask (*see* Luke 11:13) and is standing ready
to fill the needs of virtually every one of us.

Not everyone will want Jesus to fill all their needs. Many are
insisting that a marriage partner be the fulfillment. Many won't
accept the words and promise of Jesus, because they have
already predetermined that He should answer their longings in
some certain way. But by refusing to trust Jesus to be our
everything, we are asking to live in mediocrity. Many a bad
marriage has occurred when an individual couldn't trust God
to bring the very best along, and took second best in case there
were nothing better.

But if you take the chance and believe that God meant what
He said, He guarantees a life of joy and peace. In a sense,

there's a catch to it. It's that word we all shy away from—
submission. Submission to the Lord Jesus. We don't have to
know His will before we walk in it. We just have to walk,
knowing that His perfect love will not hurt us or require of us
more than we can bear.

Unconditional surrender, with no thought of the pain or the
joy, brings benefits that are beyond measure—the utterly satisfying love of the Bridegroom, our total fulfillment.

75354